# VANISHING
## PLACES

# Contents

## EUROPE



## THE AMERICAS

## AFRICA



## ASIA



## OCEANIA



## POLAR REGIONS



## OUTER SPACE

An abandoned diamond town in Namibia, once absurdly rich, is swallowed by sand. In Panama, families are forced to evacuate their sinking island home. And in Oregon, USA, the world's last Blockbuster video store fights for survival. *Vanishing Places* tells the stories of one hundred wildly different destinations that are all on the brink of disappearing.

Some are melting, crumbling, or shrinking before our eyes. Others are being altered so drastically, they risk losing every trace of what they once were. While climate change inevitably looms large, the threats explored in this book are as diverse as the places themselves. Poland's mysterious Crooked Forest fades naturally with time. Santorini's ancient vineyards, meanwhile, are bulldozed to make way for hotels.

This journey takes you to every corner of Earth – and once, even beyond it – with stories spanning sixth-century Buddhas in Afghanistan to Los Angeles neighbourhoods ravaged by wildfires in 2025. While few of us will ever set foot in Mawson's Hut, buried deep in the Antarctic wilderness, most places in this book are still within reach. A handful are best avoided for now, due to war, collapse or overwhelming crowds. All the more reason not to look away.

Though the theme of this book is loss, these pages are full of life. You'll meet the people who refuse to give up on the places they love: an Englishman using a tractor to drag his house inland as the cliff crumbles beneath it, a woman in rural Japan repopulating her deserted village with scarecrows, and a team in Tuvalu painstakingly creating a digital replica of their disappearing island.

This book is both a reflection on what we stand to lose and a reminder that, for many vanishing places, it's not too late.

# Introduction

# Europe

# Slippery slope: Switzerland's melting glaciers

**Location:**
Glaciers, Swiss Alps, particularly the Valais, Bernese Oberland and Engadine regions

**Threat:**
Climate change

In 2023, climbers crossing the Theodul glacier, above Zermatt in Switzerland, spotted something surprising: a hiking boot and crampons emerging from the ice. They had stumbled across the remains of a German climber missing since 1986. The previous year, wreckage from a plane that crashed 50 years earlier surfaced from the ice on the Alps' largest glacier, Aletsch. Many more discoveries have been made on Switzerland's glaciers in recent years, a chilling sign of how rapidly they are melting.

According to the Swiss Glacier Monitoring Network (GLAMOS), Switzerland's glaciers lost ten per cent of their total volume in just two years from 2022 to 2023 – equivalent to the total lost over three decades between 1960 and 1990. As global temperatures rise, the once towering and pristine ice is becoming thinner and greyer.

Glacial ice typically builds up in winter and melts slowly in summer, providing fresh water to Europe's rivers, crucial for irrigating crops and cooling nuclear power stations. Without the steady flow, Europe's vital systems falter. Shipping on the river Rhine, a key European waterway, had to be restricted in recent years because the water became too shallow. In 2022, fish were removed from Swiss rivers when the water became too hot and scarce.

Melting glaciers are even redrawing national borders. As ice retreats, the natural demarcations between Switzerland and Italy are shifting. In 2024, the countries were forced to renegotiate territorial lines that had been frozen in place for centuries.

Some smaller Swiss glaciers have already disappeared. GLAMOS warns that, even if global warming is curbed within the Paris Agreement's 1.5°C target, others are beyond saving. Experts predict that, without action, even the majestic Aletsch is at risk of disappearing within a generation.

# Countryside crisis: Spain's emptying villages

**Location:**
Rural regions, central and northern Spain

**Threat:**
Depopulation

"Tourists go home!" The placards held aloft by residents of Barcelona, Alicante and Seville during anti-tourism protests leave onlookers in no doubt about local feeling. Yet, while over-tourism is a serious problem in Spain's holiday hotspots, an altogether different demographic problem is wreaking havoc on the country's rural areas.

In some of Spain's agriculture-reliant regions, such as Castile and León, Extremadura and Aragón, populations are shrinking at an alarming rate. These territories, mostly in Spain's vast interior, missed out on the decades of industrialisation and development that allowed cities and tourist-friendly coastal strips to prosper. Now, as young people migrate from the countryside to the cities to find education and work, they leave behind an ageing, declining population. The threat of depopulation has given rise to a nationwide social and political movement, *La España Vaciada* (Emptied Spain), which demands help.

A province that risks being completely emptied if things don't change is Teruel in Aragon. Teruel is home to the charming historical village of Libros, which has fewer than one hundred residents, none of whom are children. The village's only teenager travels 25 kilometres to school each day. Libros's tiny but determined community is on a mission to attract tourists. Capitalising on the village's name – *Libros* is Spanish for books – locals aspire to transform Libros into a literary hub. The village's streets have been renamed after famous writers, and plans are in place to construct a 20-room hotel-library.

Government initiatives to lure outsiders to the countryside, such as tax breaks and free schooling, have had varying degrees of success. Yet rural tourism initiatives, like those in Libros, could provide a desperately-needed lifeline to the communities of La España Vaciada.

# Cliffhanger: England's crumbling coast

**Location:**
Hemsby, near Great Yarmouth, Norfolk, eastern England

**Threat:**
Coastal erosion exacerbated by storms

In 2021, British couple Marie Howlett and Tim Clarke moved to a cliff-top house in the picturesque village of Hemsby on England's Norfolk coast, fulfilling a dream of living by the sea. Two years later, however, a knock at the door brought shattering news. Marie and Tim were told that their home was at imminent risk of collapse and given just seven days to make it safe, or evacuate. Forced to abandon their furniture, deemed too dangerous to retrieve, the couple left. As Tim drove away from his home for the final time, he felt the road beginning to give way beneath him.

Coastal erosion in this part of Norfolk is a long-standing issue, and a natural process. The danger for the residents of Hemsby though, is that the growing ferocity of storms in recent years has caused erosion to advance much faster than experts predicted. Since 2013, at least twenty of Hemsby's homes have been lost – either swept into the sea or demolished as the land crumbles beneath them. Yet, one resident refused to surrender. When a 2018 storm left his house just one metre from the cliff edge, army veteran Lance Martin used a friend's tractor to haul his beloved bungalow ten metres inland.

The United Kingdom government has promised over £5 billion for flood and coastal defences by 2027, which could take the form of massive concrete walls or salt marshes acting as a protective sponge. For Hemsby, though, time is running out. In October 2024, the village was once again battered by strong winds and high tides. Residents don't know how much longer they can literally hold their ground, and fear the entire village could be lost without urgent action. Even the staunchly-defiant Lance Martin eventually decided to "up sticks", evacuating to safer terrain in November 2023 after his garden was swallowed by the sea.

# The art of endurance: France's Ice Age cave paintings

**Location:**
Lascaux cave paintings, near Montignac, Dordogne region, southwestern France

**Threat:**
Overexposure

On a warm September day in 1940, four schoolboys and their dog, Robot, roamed the Dordogne countryside, in search of adventure. It was Robot who found it, disappearing down a hole and leading the boys to an underground cave, adorned with 17,000-year-old paintings. The friends had unknowingly stumbled upon one of humanity's most significant archaeological finds, a hidden gallery that would shape our understanding of early human life.

The artists, part of an Ice Age hunter-gather community, used mineral pigments and charcoal to create nearly 600 vivid paintings and 1,500 engravings in the Lascaux Cave. Symbols with long-forgotten meanings appear alongside painted menageries of life-sized animals – horses, bison, deer, and now-extinct creatures like the woolly rhinoceros. The sophistication of the work has stunned art historians. "Since Lascaux", Picasso apparently declared upon seeing the paintings in 1940, "we have invented nothing".

The cave's unveiling sparked a wave of excitement, and in 1948, it was opened to the public. By the 1960s, more than 1,000 daily visitors crowded through its passages – bringing carbon dioxide, humidity and contaminants. The ancient murals, preserved for millennia in the dark, began to show signs of deterioration. In 1963, the cave was closed.

The years that followed saw painstaking efforts to recreate the wonders within. A meticulous partial replica called Lascaux II opened in 1983, followed by Lascaux III, which took select panels on a global tour. Since 2016, Lascaux IV has provided a full-scale replica of the cave, using 3D scanning, laser mapping and precision modelling to allow visitors to walk through a near-perfect imitation. Meanwhile, the original Lascaux Cave remains closed, its treasures carefully preserved.

# The grapes of wrath: Santorini's crushed vineyards

**Location:**
Santorini vineyards, volcanic slopes of Santorini, southern Aegean Sea, Greece

**Threat:**
Overdevelopment

Since long before Santorini became Insta-famous, ancient vineyards have clung to the island's volcanic slopes. Santorini's vines are some of the oldest in the world. They are grown in a basket shape on the ground, a centuries-old method of protecting them from the strong sun and wind.

Over the last 60 years, Santorini's vineyards have been flattened by the relentless march of tourism. Farms have steadily been replaced by villa complexes and hotels for the 3.4 million tourists who descend each year. In the 1960s, Santorini had 3,000 hectares of vines; today, there are fewer than 1,000. A calamitous 82 percent drop in grape production was recorded in 2024, exacerbated by droughts and scorching temperatures. Meanwhile, vineyard workers have left in their droves, drawn to more lucrative and comfortable hospitality jobs.

Santorini is widely known to be buckling under the weight of its own popularity. Despite the well-documented crisis of overtourism on the island, "Santorini honeymoon" was still one of Google's most searched terms in 2024. On peak days, more than 10,000 cruise passengers disembark, putting an almost unbearable strain on the island's infrastructure, ecosystems and residents. For over a decade, the mayor of Santorini has pleaded for restrictions on cruise ships and construction, but decisions rest with Athens. There are plans to finally enforce a daily limit of 8,000 cruise passengers in 2025.

Winemakers urge the government to protect the remaining vineyards and address water shortages. Santorini's vineyards may not be as iconic as its whitewashed buildings and blue domed churches, but their loss would sever an important part of the island's identity. Innovative solutions are being trialled, like using wastewater for irrigation. By focusing on sustainability and clamping down on mass tourism, Santorini's ancient vines may continue to grow.

# Out on a limb: Poland's crooked forest

**Location:**
Crooked Forest, Nowe Czarnowo village, near Gryfino, northwest Poland

**Threat:**
Ageing

In a quiet corner of western Poland, near the town of Gryfino, there is a grove of pines unlike any other. Their trunks all bend sharply north, like dancers frozen mid-bow. Planted around 1930 over 0.5 hectares, the trees in Poland's Crooked Forest seem to defy nature.

No one knows for sure why the trees bend, with theories spanning folklore and science. Some say tanks rumbled over them in 1945, stunting their growth, while others whisper of electromagnetic fields and underground water veins. The most plausible explanation points to human intervention. Foresters perhaps shaped the trees to create curved wood for furniture or sleighs, a theory backed up by the symmetrical planting arrangement.

In 1971, there were 400 pines in the Crooked Forest. The 100 that remain are now nearly a century old, approaching the end of their natural lifespans. Though pines can live up to 300 years, the curved trees face additional pressures. The growing popularity of the Crooked Forest, fuelled by social media, has led to an influx of tourists who climb and sit on branches, unwittingly weakening them in the process.

The Crooked Forest is now protected as a Polish natural monument, and efforts to preserve its legacy are taking root. In 2021, the forest's legal caretakers, Gryfino Forest District, planted 1,000 new pines in two nearby areas. Half of these saplings were grown from seeds of the original trees and will grow naturally. The other half will be carefully shaped by foresters, to replicate the iconic curves of the original forest.

In a few years, visitors will see the new generation starting to take shape. As the original trees bow to time, their successors will grow, perhaps bringing an answer to the enduring mystery – was the Crooked Forest crafted by human hands, or by nature?

# Glory days: England's fading seaside towns

**Location:**
Towns along nearly all of England's coast, notably Jaywick Sands in Essex, Blackpool in Lancashire, Great Yarmouth in Norfolk and Hastings in East Sussex

**Threat:**
Deindustralization, economic decline

The seaside town is a powerful motif in the British shared imagination, immortalized in countless films and novels as a symbol of past glory and nostalgia. England's once buzzing coastal resorts still promote themselves as places to enjoy life's simple pleasures: rock pooling, amusement arcades and ice cream on the pier. Yet, for locals, life beside the seaside is often marred by deprivation.

From Clacton in the east to Weston-super-Mare in the west, a pattern of economic and social decline has taken root in towns along England's coast. From the 1960s, the surge in cheap overseas holidays led to the steady decline of English seaside resorts. The problem was exacerbated by limited job prospects beyond low-paid hospitality work and a housing market that increasingly favoured second-home buyers and holiday lets.

Despite these setbacks, England's famous seaside spots still attract impressive visitor numbers, with ten million tourists flocking to Blackpool alone every year. The post-Covid home working revolution has brought new opportunities, and a rising cost of living has pushed more and more families out of the cities in search of affordable lifestyles. Seaside towns are already enjoying the benefits. Ramsgate in Kent, once dismissed as shabby, has been resurrected as an arty hipster hotspot.

Pockets of investment offer a brighter future for some areas. A new attraction, Eden Project Morecambe, has been awarded £50 million in the United Kingdom Government's Levelling Up Fund. Expected to open on the Lancashire coast in 2028, the exhibition aims to reimagine Morecambe as a seaside resort for the 21st century. Projects like these – along with hundreds of creative community projects – offer an inspiring vision of new ways to enjoy England's seaside.

# Drowning in popularity: Venice

**Location:**
Venice, northeastern Italy

**Threat:**
Overtourism

Few places illustrate the impact of unchecked tourism as vividly as Venice. Over five million visitors – mostly day-trippers – pour into the historic city every year, causing a litany of environmental problems and making life almost intolerable for residents. In peak season, gondolas jostle for canal space, while locals report struggling to push prams along streets clogged with tourists. The relentless crowds have contributed to a mass exodus of residents, reducing central Venice's population from over 125,000 in the 1960s to fewer than 50,000 today.

With Venetians departing, the city has turned its attention to tourism, leaving Venice struggling to hold onto its authenticity and infrastructure. UNESCO warned in 2023 that Venice's historic centre was facing irreversible damage. The authorities listened. In April 2024, Venice became the world's first city to charge day-trippers to enter on select days. The entry fee of €5 (£4.30) and a series of new rules – including banning loudspeakers and limiting tour groups – followed a 2021 ban on cruise ships entering the city centre.

Critics argue the entry fee does little more than reduce Venice to a theme park. While it raised millions in 2024, the toll failed to curb numbers, with some fee-paying days attracting 10,000 more tourists than the previous year. Local campaigners demand long-term solutions, including stricter regulation on holiday-lets, improved services for locals, and education for tourists, to remind them that Venice is also a home.

Venice has long been seen by other tourism hotspots as a guinea pig for tackling overtourism. The world watches as the Italian authorities experiment with measures to ease the strain on the fragile floating city, in search of the elusive balance between tourism and local life.

ГОТЕЛЬ

# Call of the wild: the Ukrainian city frozen in time

Pripyat was built in 1970 to house workers from the nearby Chernobyl Nuclear Power Plant and their families. For sixteen years, it thrived as a typical Soviet city. Then, on Saturday, 26 April 1986, everything changed. Reactor No. 4 at Chernobyl suffered a catastrophic explosion, igniting a fire that spewed radioactive material across the surrounding area.

The next day, Pripyat's 50,000 residents were ordered to evacuate. It was a bright spring morning and birds sang overhead as families boarded buses, hastily leaving their homes and possessions behind. The residents believed they would return in a few days, but as the scale of the disaster unfolded, it became clear they would never be coming back. That day, Pripyat was frozen in time. The city's clocks still show the time the electricity was cut on the day of the evacuation, children's toys lie scattered and the ferris wheel – set to open one week after the explosion – is motionless.

Today, the city is part of the 30-kilometre exclusion zone that surrounds Chernobyl. Nature has reclaimed much of the land in the zone, and wolves, wild horses, boars and lynx are among the creatures that roam freely. Largely unaffected by radiation poisoning, these animals are thriving without human interference. Tourists drawn to Pripyat's eerie beauty and history were once allowed short visits, prior to the Russian invasion of Ukraine. Russia occupied the exclusion zone briefly in early 2022 and, in March 2023, it was closed to visitors, leaving Pripyat to be reclaimed by nature.

Though many buildings have decayed, vegetation has woven itself through the cracks, and ecosystems have developed in surprising ways, offering scientists valuable insights into how wildlife adapts and regenerates. In Pripyat, life has found a way to thrive, even in the shadow of human tragedy.

**Location:**
Pripyat, near Chernobyl, northern Ukraine

**Threat:**
Abandonment

# Mother of all traditions: Europe's Island of Women

**Location:**
Kihnu Island, Baltic Sea, off western Estonia

**Threat:**
Migration

As evening draws in, a woman sews at her kitchen table. This is not the only work her capable hands have done that day – she has tended chickens and sheep, cooked for her children and repaired a tractor motor.

This woman lives on Kihnu, a small Estonian island in the Baltic Sea. Known as the Island of Women, it is powered by the hands of mothers, sisters and aunts. Kihnu's women educate children and uphold ancestral traditions. They farm, conduct weddings, and bury their dead.

Men have been historically absent, hunting seals at sea or working abroad, and the role of women has expanded into every corner of life. Kihnu is often referred to as Europe's Last Matriarchy, although locals prefer the term matrifocal. They point out that, while women keep the gears running on the island – literally and figuratively – men's work is important for sustaining island culture.

Kihnu's unique way of life goes back hundreds, if not thousands, of years and in 2008 it was inscribed on UNESCO's Intangible Cultural Heritage List. Women are custodians of the island's traditions, passing on stories, folk songs and artisan skills to their daughters. Their bright embroidered clothing is a defining part of their culture, and the colour of a woman's skirt signifies whether she is single, married or mourning. Traditional skirts are still worn today, sometimes paired with an Apple Watch.

Kihnu's women are resilient, but the island's future is precarious. Youngsters leave in search of opportunities, while the ageing population dwindles, and fishing and farming are increasingly difficult to sustain. The survival of Europe's Island of Women depends on shaping a future that balances tradition with modern life; a future that appeals to Kihnu's growing girls.

# Last catch: Iceland's abandoned herring factory

**Location:**
Djúpavík village in Árneshreppur municipality, Westfjords, northwestern Iceland

**Threat:**
Deindustralization

Few drives rival the drama of a road trip through the remote Árneshreppur municipality in Iceland's Westfjords. The landscape's towering cliffs, deep fjords and mountains are punctuated by tiny settlements. Among them is creekside Djúpavík, home to just four people.

The village was established in 1917, when a herring factory opened. A second reiteration of the factory was built in 1934 and became the largest concrete building in Iceland at the time. Catches were almost unlimited and, for a while, the booming herring industry transformed the lives of the local community. However, by the 1940s, stocks started to dwindle rapidly. Despite several attempts to repurpose it, the factory closed in 1954.

The village of Djúpavík now faces the same fate as Iceland's far north. The once populated region was deserted during waves of migration, and the land is now inhabited by more Arctic foxes than humans. Djúpavík's tiny community is doing what it can to encourage visitors. The old herring factory has been converted into a museum and exhibition space, used as the venue for a Sigur Rós music concert in 2006. While the houses in Djúpavík are occupied only in summer, the village's lone hotel, which once housed factory workers, is open all year.

According to 2025 data, there are just 62 residents in Árneshreppur, making it Iceland's lowest-populated municipality. Public transport is non-existent, and the snaking dirt roads can be tough going. Yet, those willing to try the road less travelled are richly rewarded, as the Westfjords are arguably more dramatic than their easterly counterparts. Árneshreppur is one of Iceland's most striking places, where few tourists reach, and Djúpavík village offers a rare opportunity for a traveller to feel worlds away.

# Coasting along: Denmark's moving lighthouse

**Location:**
Rubjerg Knude Lighthouse, Jutland Peninsula, northwestern Denmark

**Threat:**
Coastal erosion

For 125 years, the Rubjerg Knude lighthouse has perched on a clifftop on Denmark's northern coast, but it hasn't always stood in the same spot.

The 23-metre brick tower, topped by a red lantern room, was built in 1900 on Rubjerg Knude's cliffs, 60 metres above the North Sea. Decommissioned in 1968, it now draws 250,000 tourists to the sand dunes on Denmark's Jutland peninsula each year.

The idea of the lighthouse ever falling into the sea would probably have seemed absurd to its builders, as the coast was then 200 metres away and showed little sign of receding. However, in time, the sea began to devour the shoreline at a rate of around two metres per year.

When a nearby coastal church was dismantled in 2008, to prevent it from collapsing into the water, attention turned to the lighthouse, which was only a few metres from the edge. Basic calculations suggested it would topple within two years. After much deliberation, officials approved a £0.6 million government-funded plan to move the lighthouse. Local mason, Kjeld Pedersen, was entrusted with the task. "I might as well say it as it is", he told a Danish newspaper. "I've never moved a lighthouse before."

Nevertheless, in October 2019, global media outlets reported from the Danish coast, as Pedersen's team lifted the 720-tonne structure, placed it on parallel rails, and moved it 70 metres inland, at a cautious pace of eight metres per hour. The Mayor acknowledged that much could have gone wrong during the process, but the operation was a success. After an inauguration party to mark its safe arrival at its new location, the lighthouse reopened to the public.

If current calculations are correct, the Rubjerg Knude lighthouse should remain secure until at least 2060, after which, it may be on the move once again.

# Suspended: Northern England's broken bridge

**Location:**
Tees Transporter Bridge, spanning the River Tees, near Middlesbrough, in northern England

**Threat:**
Structural deterioration

In 1974, English comedian Terry Scott, known for his roles in seven *Carry On* films, misread a road sign and drove his Jaguar off the end of the Tees Transporter Bridge. Thankfully, he landed in the safety netting beneath, rather than in the freezing river.

Built in 1911, the Tees Transporter Bridge in northern England was once the world's longest transporter bridge, meaning it ferries vehicles and pedestrians across the River Tees on a suspended gondola. As long as three football pitches and known locally as "The Transporter", it has long been a proud symbol of England's northeast. Yet, Terry Scott's driving mishap is just one chapter in the bridge's troubled history.

It was damaged by bombing during World War II and suffered a notorious malfunction in 1953, when the gondola became stranded mid-route amid gale-force winds. In recent years, the bridge's condition has worsened significantly. In 2019, it was temporarily closed after a whistleblower warned it was structurally dangerous. A subsequent probe revealed that a worker had narrowly escaped being killed when a piece of the structure fell. Worse still, a 2024 report found the bridge to be at risk of "catastrophic collapse" and cautioned that, if repairs are not carried out, an exclusion zone will have to be placed around it.

The British government has allocated £30 million to restore the bridge, but experts predict that the real cost will be closer to £67 million. There has been a proposal to turn the bridge into a leisure attraction, which was met with public outcry. Local politicians and residents are united in a fight for the Tees Transporter Bridge to one day carry passengers again, as it did for over 100 years. For now though, this remarkable Edwardian landmark remains closed, its future hanging in the balance.

# Italy's dying town: Civita di Bagnoregio

**Location:**
Civita di Bagnoregio, near Lake Bolsena, Lazio region, central Italy

**Threat:**
Erosion

The medieval village of Civita di Bagnoregio perches on a rocky outcrop, tethered to the modern world by a long narrow footbridge. When morning mist settles in the canyon below, the village remains visible above it, creating the illusion that it's floating on clouds.

To cross the bridge is to enter a place suspended in time. The village's medieval buildings have remarkably well-preserved stone facades, arched doorways and terracotta rooftops. Stone hoops still cling to the sides of buildings, where horses were once tethered. This compact maze of cobblestone streets has withstood 2,500 years of historical and natural challenges. Over time, relentless wind and rain have carved away at the rocky plateau. Parts of the village teeter on the brink of collapse, earning it the nickname "The Dying Town".

Civita di Bagnoregio is inhabited by just a handful of residents, but as word of its fragile beauty spreads, more and more travellers, academics and artists make their way across the bridge to the village. It is both frozen in time and yet ever changing, as the landscape is constantly reshaped by landslides. Information panels in the village's tiny museum reveal that the valley floor has moved 40 metres since 1764.

Over the past 35 years, work has been done to stabilise the land, reinforce structures and prevent further landslides, but more is needed. The village is under consideration by UNESCO to be granted World Heritage Site status, which would bring welcome attention and resources. Civita di Bagnoregio is locked in a battle with nature, but the dying town is determined to live on.

# Field of dreams: Berlin's repurposed runways

**Location:**
Tempelhof Field, Tempelhof-Schöneberg district, Berlin, Germany

**Threat:**
Redevelopment

Tempelhof Field, a public park in south-central Berlin, is a rare example of sprawling openness in a busy city. The 384-hectare green space was once a historic airfield, but now cyclists and skateboarders glide down the vast empty runways. For Berliners, the space is a shared garden. On sunny days, around 25,000 people turn up to jog, fly kites, tend community gardens, or simply escape the city. Tempelhof is more than a park – it's a place of connection, a creative and cultural hub, where art installations and pop-up events flourish.

Tempelhof was once very different. The airport opened in 1923 and became the site of several historic events. Its two runways served as a lifeline during the 1948/49 Berlin Airlift, when Western Allies defied Stalin's blockade to land supply planes at Tempelhof every 60 seconds. Tempelhof's aviation activity came to an end when the airport closed in 2008, its runways unable to cope with modern jets. By 2010, the airfield had been reinvented as one of the city's most treasured community spaces and an emblem for Berliners' creativity and resilience.

The area has been protected from change since 2014 by a law passed by a majority of Berliners in a referendum. However, since the referendum, Berlin's housing crisis has worsened, reigniting the debate about the future of Tempelhof. The government's proposal to develop parts of the field have met fierce resistance, with campaigners arguing that other spaces in the city could be used to meet housing needs.

The government organised an ideas competition for architects and designers' proposals, but this only deepened divisions. Undeterred, campaigners continue to fight for Tempelhof to live on as an open space where Berliners' spirits are free to soar.

Screen
Machine
Scotland's Mobile Cinema
Taigh-dhealbh Siùbhlach na h-Alba
www.screenmachine.co.uk
Follow us on

# That's a wrap: Scotland's community cinema

From the day it opened in the 1930s, the Oban Phoenix Cinema has served as a community hub for the small coastal town of Oban – not to mention a refuge from the often blustery weather. Naturally, it provided plenty of entertainment too, with its two screens (one with just 22 seats) showing everything from blockbusters to live-streamed theatre.

However, cinema audiences dwindled over the years and, in 2010, the Oban Phoenix came close to shutting. Fortunately for the cinema, one of its regulars happened to be an Oscar-winning actor. Dame Judi Dench joined the campaign to save the picture house and the community rallied, raising funds to purchase and renovate the building.

The Phoenix rose as a symbol of Oban's fighting spirit and in 2012 the cinema reopened as a community-owned business and local charity. It remained a cornerstone of Oban's community for over a decade, after which its owners again struggled to balance the books. In 2024, the cinema was forced into liquidation and put up for sale, with cinema bosses blaming declining customer numbers since the pandemic, combined with rising operating costs.

Since 2024, Dame Judi Dench has also been urging Scotland's First Minister to help prevent the loss of Screen Machine, a 80-seat cinema bus that travels around the country's highlands and islands. Like Oban's cinema, Screen Machine faces financial challenges that jeopardise its future, but Dench maintains the mobile cinema is a lifeline to rural communities.

Local supporters could not alleviate the cash flow problems of their beloved cinema, but they remain hopeful that the Oban Phoenix will attract a buyer who believes as passionately as they do in the power of community cinema.

**Location:**
Oban Phoenix Cinema, Oban, Argyll and Bute, west coast of Scotland

**Threat:**
Financial challenges

# Boom to bust: Russia's ravaged monotowns

**Location:**
Russia's monotowns, primarily Siberia and Urals region, Russia

**Threat:**
Economic decline

Relics of Soviet industrial ambition, Russia's monotowns are places whose economy is built around a single industry, sometimes even a single factory. Around thirteen million people – almost one in ten Russians – live and work in the country's 319 or so monotowns. Most developed around heavy industries like coal, oil and metals, and life in these towns can be as harsh as the isolated landscapes they occupy. In the coal-mining monotown of Vorkuta, just north of the Arctic Circle, temperatures plunge to -50°C.

Russia's transition to a market economy in the early 1990s caused widespread problems for its once-thriving monotowns. Unemployment rocketed to twice the national average and, to this day, the residents grapple with poor infrastructure, education and health. The towns' remote locations and pricey airfares make it almost impossible to travel. If someone from an isolated monotown makes it onto a flight, they usually don't plan to come back.

In 2009, several hundred residents from Pikalyovo, a small industrial monotown in Leningrad Oblast, blocked the highway in protest against months of unpaid work. The privately-owned factories they worked in ground to a halt. It took a visit from Vladimir Putin for production to finally resume, and the incident laid bare the precariousness of monotowns' dependence on single industries.

Despite the decline of monotowns, the government has resisted closing factories, fearing social and political instability. However, it has allocated funds to diversify and develop local economies, and corporations have invested in tourism and infrastructure projects. According to government classifications, eighteen towns have now shed their monotown status, by embracing new industries and entrepreneurial growth. Yet, many more still teeter between survival and obscurity.

# Stone cold crisis: The ancient cleits of St Kilda

**Location:**
St Kilda, 66km off Outer Hebrides, western Scotland

**Threat:**
Droughts caused by climate change

The islands of the St Kilda archipelago, perched 66 kilometres off Scotland's Outer Hebrides, are nicknamed the "islands at the edge of the world". It's hard to imagine how anyone ever lived there, but St Kilda was inhabited from the Bronze Age until the last residents left in 1930. Today, it is a windswept remnant of a bygone way of life.

St Kilda was once home to Britain's most remote island community, whose life was shaped by extreme isolation and a rugged environment. Residents endured howling Atlantic storms and survived on seabirds and fish. A legacy of their lifestyle remains in the cleits that are scattered across St Kilda. These centuries-old, beehive-shaped stone chambers were used to cure fish and store bird carcasses, eggs and crops. They were built so that wind passes straight though, aiding preservation.

The climate on St Kilda has changed dramatically in recent years. The once rain-swept isles now experience periods of drought. In summer 2023, visitors were encouraged to bring their own drinking water as island supplies were running low. Droughts are believed to be disrupting the foundations of the dry stone cleits and accelerating their collapse. The National Trust for Scotland (NTS) owns St Kilda and, with limited funds, faces the unenviable task of deciding which cleits to save. It is estimated that up to two thirds of the 1,400 or so structures will be left to collapse.

Descendants of St Kildan residents fundraise from afar to help fund the NTS's conservation work, but the remoteness of the archipelago makes conservation efforts far more complicated and expensive than they would be on the mainland. Many of the cleits will almost certainly succumb to nature, but those that are saved will stand as monuments to the resilient communities who once called St Kilda home.

MARKS & SPENCER
MARKS & SPENCER
M&S
M&S
M&S
CLINIQUE
M&S

# Destined for demolition: London's doomed Art Deco icon

Marks & Spencer, or M&S as it's fondly known by shoppers, has been a popular British retailer of food, fashion and homewares since 1884. The brand's flagship store is a stately, geometric Art Deco building dating back to the 1930s – an architectural landmark of London's iconic Oxford Street.

Change is on the horizon for the historic building. After a tumultuous four-year legal battle, the retailer has been given permission by the British government to flatten the premises, called Orchard House, and replace it with a ten-storey building containing shops, a café, a gym and offices.

The demolition has been fiercely opposed on the grounds of both heritage and sustainability. Objections have been raised by conservation groups, architects, engineers and public figures, including author Bill Bryson. The proposal has sparked a debate that extends beyond Orchard House, with the case becoming a lightning rod for the predicament that cities everywhere are grappling with: tear down historic buildings, or try to reuse and retrofit them?

After nearly a century as part of Oxford Street's landscape, Orchard House must prepare for its final chapter. The conversation it triggered about sustainability, heritage and progress, however, will rumble on long after the wrecking ball has swung. Times have been hard for Britain's high streets and, while many people will mourn the loss of a nostalgic London landmark, the demolition of the M&S store is a chance for developers to breathe new life into the UK's most famous shopping street.

**Location:**
Marks & Spencer department store, Oxford Street, central London, England

**Threat:**
Redevelopment

# Deerly departed: Lapland's ruined reindeer habitats

**Location:**
Sámi reindeer-herding region, spanning Lapland and northwestern Russia

**Threat:**
Climate change, human expansion

Every summer, hundreds of thousands of reindeer are guided by herders on a journey from the highlands of northern Europe to the coastal tundra. The annual reindeer migration is a tradition upheld for thousands of years by the Indigenous people of Lapland, called Sámi. Numbering around 80,000, the Sámi have a deep connection to the land, passed down since the end of the last Ice Age and woven into their identity.

Yet, as the Arctic warms up at an alarming rate – some scientists say up to four times faster than the global average – the Sámi's delicate bond with nature is under threat. The fluctuating climate is wreaking havoc on their environment. The once-predictably fluffy snow is changing and now often forms dense, icy layers that the reindeer struggle to dig through.

Though the Sámi have more than 300 words for different types of snow and ice conditions, they have no word for this new variety. Unable to break through with their hooves to unearth lichen and fungi, the reindeer scatter further in search of food, pulling their herders with them.

Adding to these challenges, reindeer habitats are being carved up by logging and mining activities, and increasing rainfall makes the lichen they eat soggy and less nutritious. Pushed to the brink, reindeer populations have suffered mass starvations, including a major loss in 2018-19, on the Norwegian archipelago of Svalbard.

The Sámi people's existence depends on the delicate symbiosis between nature, weather and reindeer populations. Fighting for the survival of their homeland and livelihoods, they are taking political action against the industrial forces and legislation that threaten them. Without protection, the Sámi's irreplaceable ecological knowledge, reindeer herding traditions, and the very land they inhabit will be lost.

# The Americas

# Derailed: Mexico's unstable underground world

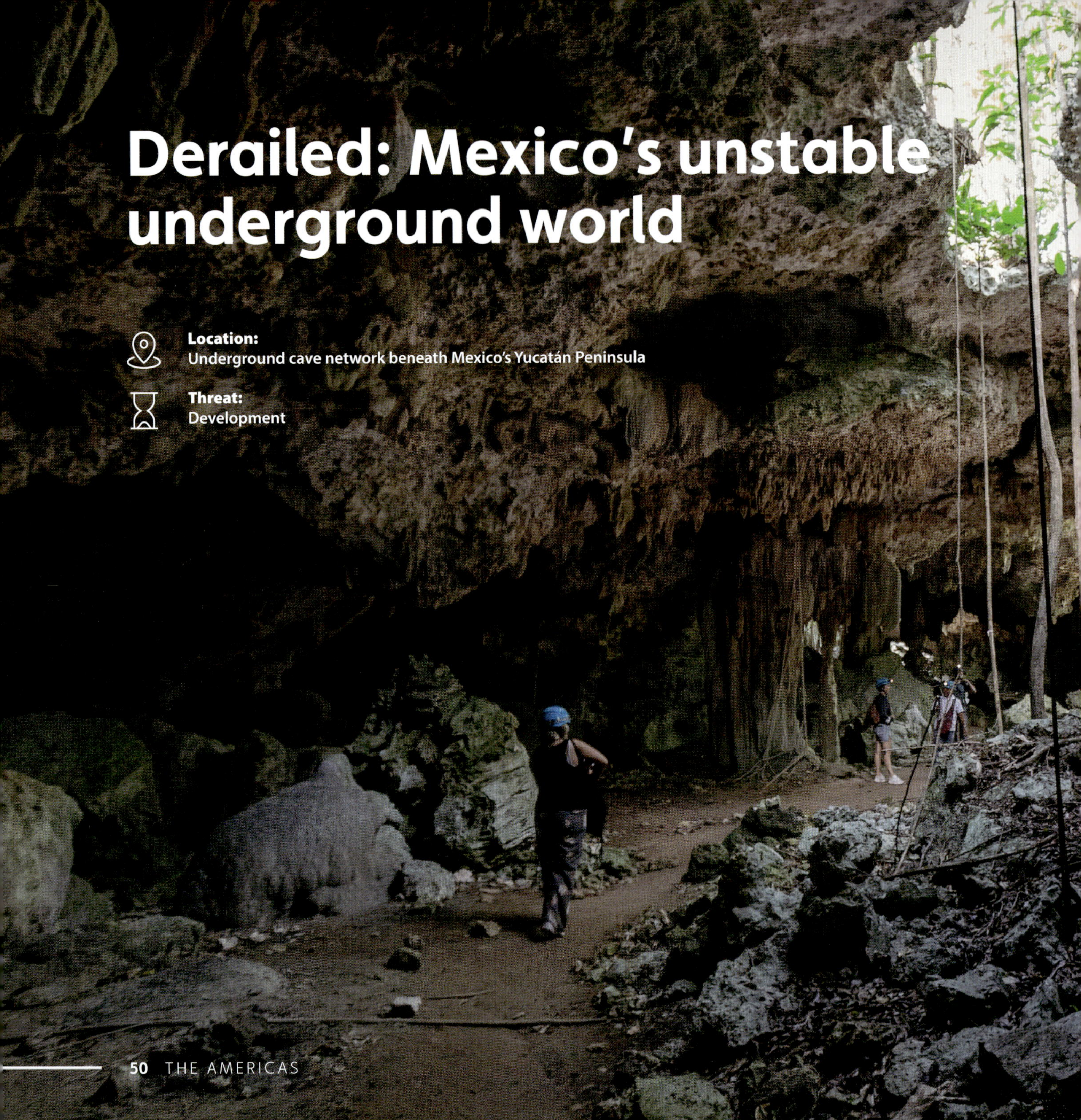

**Location:**
Underground cave network beneath Mexico's Yucatán Peninsula

**Threat:**
Development

Beneath Mexico's eastern Yucatán Peninsula lies a hidden labyrinth of caves, sinkholes and underground rivers carved out over millions of years. As well as supporting unique ecosystems, the fragile cave system holds some of the world's clearest freshwater and the region's main water source – but it is at risk.

Tren Maya was the flagship infrastructure project of Mexico's former President Andrés Manuel López Obrador. The tourist railway line, which opened fully in 2024, loops around Mexico's southern Yucatan Peninsula. President López Obrador said that pillars used to elevate the train would protect the caves below, but critics argue the steel columns have done the opposite.

Geologists have compared the fragile and cavity-riddled underground world to gruyere cheese. To embed the estimated 15,000 steel pillars, biologists believe that massive drills were used to bore into the limestone. Since construction, there have been reports of broken stalactites found strewn across the cave system – victims of underground landslides caused by trains thundering overhead.

Scientists also report that concrete has spilled from pillars, coating the ground, and that cave water shows signs of iron pollution. Greenpeace Mexico warns of biodiversity loss, as the caves are home to bats and blind cavefish, and even a refuge for jaguars seeking drinking water.

Environmental campaigners succeeded in temporarily suspending construction, due to the lack of environmental permits. However, President López Obrador dismissed critics, declaring the project a matter of national security. Despite protests, his government and that of his successor, President Sheinbaum, proceeded with the development. Now, a growing coalition of scientists, environmentalists and cavers fight to save the Yucatán's underground world, so that its story – millennia old – does not end here.

# The Pompeii of the Caribbean: Plymouth, Montserrat

**Location:**
Plymouth, Montserrat, Leeward Islands, Caribbean

**Threat:**
Volcanic activity

The mountainous island of Montserrat is the world's only political territory to have a ghost town as its legal capital. It's hard to believe this largely deserted island was once a place synonymous with a booming economy and luxury holidays, nicknamed "The Emerald Isle of the Caribbean".

In 1995, after laying dormant for centuries, the Soufrière Hills volcano on the southern part of the island erupted. This marked the start of a series of catastrophic volcanic events that lasted for more than a decade, transforming the swanky A-list haunt into the Caribbean's answer to Pompeii. Montserrat's capital, Plymouth, was eventually abandoned for good in 1997, after a series of eruptions that year destroyed most of the city.

This fifteen-year period of volcanic activity rendered half of Montserrat uninhabitable and led to a large portion of the population fleeing the island. Much of the island's southern side now falls under an apocalyptic-sounding exclusion zone, deemed too dangerous to visit, while Plymouth remains buried under a mountain of volcanic ash. Attempts to repair the island were largely unsuccessful, until the 2019 launch of the Montserrat Port Development Project, an ambitious rescue scheme funded by £28 million in UK grants. In 2022, ground was finally broken and the construction of Montserrat's new capital began.

Tours of the buried city of Plymouth resumed in 2024, although intrepid travellers are advised to explore the site with caution. In the same year, it was reported that scientists from Oxford University believe that fluids beneath the dormant volcano may have the potential to make geothermal energy a viable source of renewable energy. Their ongoing scientific investigation, together with the return of safe and sensible tourism, could hold the key to the island's salvation.

# Trampled: Machu Picchu in peril

**Location:**
Machu Picchu, Andes Mountains, southern Peru

**Threat:**
Overtourism

In 2024, a tourist visiting Peru made headlines for all the wrong reasons, when a viral video appeared to show her scattering ashes over Machu Picchu. The violation sparked outrage and shone a spotlight on the heavy toll excessive tourism takes on the sacred site.

Built by the Incas in the fifteenth century, Machu Picchu is a wonder of architecture and engineering, and a UNESCO World Heritage Site. The ancient city features precisely crafted walls and terraces, thousands of granite steps and over 200 stone buildings, all built without using wheels, high in the Andes.

Machu Picchu is one of South America's most popular tourist destinations, drawing 1.4 million visitors every year, expected to rise to 1.6 million in 2025. While tourism brings vital revenue to the rural region, it also causes significant damage. Machu Picchu's narrow pathways and fragile ecosystems are overwhelmed by the unrelenting tide of visitors. Local families are crowded out by souvenir shops and tourist amenities, while communities and wildlife are disturbed by helicopter tours and litter, and infrastructure buckles under the strain.

In response to UNESCO's threat to put Machu Picchu on its list of endangered places, Peruvian authorities implemented strict new measures. Tourists can only visit select areas, during assigned time slots, and cannot stay longer than four hours. Daily visitors have been capped at 4,500 per day, or 5,600 in peak season (the citadel was likely built for around 750 people). Peruvian authorities are optimistic that these measures balance preservation with accessibility. Machu Picchu, they say, continues to welcome travellers who are responsible, respectful and who leave no trace – ashes included.

# Survival stories: Africatown, Alabama

**Location:**
Africatown, Mobile, Alabama, southern USA

**Threat:**
Neglect, environmental hazards

In the spring of 1860, 110 enslaved men, women and children were forced to board a schooner named *Clotilda* and smuggled from Africa to the port city of Mobile, Alabama. The trafficking of enslaved people had been outlawed 53 years earlier, and the venture was the result of a wager between two wealthy white men. It was the last known voyage of enslaved Africans to the United States.

Five years after the *Clotilda* docked in Alabama, slavery was abolished. Unable to return to Africa, the people enslaved on the *Clotilda* settled in the US, eventually finding manual work and buying land. Their settlement, in which they appointed leaders and communicated in their native languages, came to be known as Africatown. It still exists today – one of the few American communities created by West Africans who survived the Middle Passage.

Over time, more majority-Black neighbourhoods clustered around Africatown and the area became industrialized. Today, the neighbourhood is ensconced by heavy manufacturing hubs, and Africatown residents are plagued with health concerns caused by industrial pollution. The rapid urbanisation of Mobile threatens to erode the neighbourhood's character, and residents fear being displaced by gentrification.

The *Clotilda* was burnt by slavers and lost to history, until archaeologists located the wreck in the muddy waters of Mobile Bay in 2019. This discovery gave new life to an ongoing campaign to establish Africatown as a place of heritage tourism. In 2023, the Africatown Heritage House museum opened a new £1 million exhibition, chronicling the legacy of the community. Residents and allies strive to find ways for Africatown to prosper, without weakening its cultural identity. The arrival of more tourists, seeking education and truth, is part of the answer.

# Flatlining: Bolivia's fragile salt flat

A magnet for travellers with a knack for smartphone photography, Bolivia's Salar de Uyuni is the Earth's largest and most mesmerizing salt flat. It's approximately the size of Jamaica and perched 3,656 metres above sea level on an Andean plateau. When it floods, the great white expanse becomes an otherworldly mirror of the sky. Its flat featureless surface eliminates depth perception, making objects and people appear miniscule or gigantic, and travellers spend hours creating bizarre optical illusions. However, below the eerily beautiful surface, trouble is brewing.

The shifting climate is putting the salt flat in an increasingly precarious position. Rising temperatures and precipitation can affect water levels and lead to erosion of the salt crust. If that wasn't enough to contend with, Salar de Uyuni is believed to be sitting on a quarter of the world's lithium reserves. As demand for batteries for electric cars and smartphones booms, the Bolivian government is keen (to put it mildly) to tap into its resources. Lithium extraction typically involves pumping brine into large ponds and retrieving the crystalised lithium salts once the water has evaporated. Bolivia's state-owned mining company opened its first industrial-scale lithium plant near Uyuni in 2023.

While supporters have hailed Bolivia the "Saudi Arabia of lithium" and the government has its sights set on a bumper payday, critics are asking, at what cost? The full impact of lithium mining is yet to be seen, but it's likely that lithium production facilities will draw heavily on the region's water sources. Locals, including llama herders and quinoa farmers, are anxious about water shortages and the impact of mining on the salt flat's delicate ecosystem. While lithium might be white gold in the eyes of the government, without cautious and sustainable mining practices, Bolivia's dreamlike salt flat risks becoming the stuff of legend.

**Location:**
Salar de Uyuni, Potosí and Oruro departments, southwestern Bolivia

**Threat:**
Lithium mining and climate change

# Unravelling: Peru's woven histories

**Location:**
The Andes, southern Peru

**Threat:**
Modernization

High in the Peruvian Andes, Quechua women use tools made from wood and llama bone to weave scenes of meandering rivers and soaring condors into colourful fabric. Through textiles, they tell the stories of their lives and their land, just as their ancestors have done for centuries.

Peru's Quechua people are descendants of the Inca Empire. The remoteness of the country's southern region has helped their communities preserve age-old textile techniques. More than a technical skill, weaving is a sacred tradition that connects them to their ancestors. In traditional Quechua societies, it is even favoured above writing as a form of expression; intricate designs are a visual vocabulary passed from mothers to daughters.

As with many forms of Indigenous expertise, it is often the elders in Quechua communities who are the masters of the craft. The survival of their weaving traditions relies on finding willing apprentices among the younger generations, which is not always easy. The rise of cheap, machine-made textiles poses a further threat to the traditional artform.

Yet the Quechua people are resilient. Their ancestral traditions have survived centuries of change and there's every reason to believe they can endure the latest wave of modernisation. Quechua communities are welcoming tourists for weaving demonstrations and textile sales. More importantly, young people are stepping forward to become students of the craft. By learning to weave using traditional methods, the apprentices are helping to preserve their people's ancestral stories, one thread at a time.

# Ripple effect: the unlikely hero of Louisiana's coast

**Location:**
Grand Bayou village, marshlands of Mississippi River Delta, Plaquemines Parish, Louisiana, southern USA

**Threat:**
Coastal erosion

A century ago, Grand Bayou village in the Mississippi River Delta was home to around 1,000 people. Today, only fourteen families of the Atakapa-Ishak Chawasha Indigenous community remain, their homes accessible only by boat.

Residents recall idyllic childhoods on the bayou (a slow-moving, swampy river), when their community was largely self-sustaining. Now, the village is slowly dissolving into the sea, making life precarious. Land erosion and saltwater intrusion have hindered farming, and the salt-infused riverbank is haunted by withered remains of great oaks, which locals say are the bones of the forest that once grew there.

Both natural and man-made factors are to blame. Canals have been carved through the marsh for oil exploration and flood control, disrupting the Mississippi River's natural flow and starving the delta of vital sediment. Rising sea levels and increasing intense storms, fuelled by climate change, have made things worse.

The remaining villagers have partnered with an environmental non-profit group, the Coalition to Restore Coastal Louisiana, to harness the power of a humble hero: the oyster. Volunteers collect recycled shells from restaurants, haul the 14kg sacks onto boats, and stack them along the bayou's fragile banks. The strategically placed shells form a natural barrier against the waves, slowing erosion.

This simple, low-tech solution has had remarkable results. Over 3,000 metres of oyster reef have been installed since 2014, reducing shoreline erosion by up to 50 percent in similar areas. The bayou's reefs are now thriving ecosystems, attracting fish, crabs and birds, and reviving fishing opportunities. Shell by shell, volunteers remind the people of Grand Bayou that they have not been forgotten.

VANISHING
CULTURAL
PRACTICE
332

# Living legacy: America's Native culture under siege

Census data shows that, since the start of the 21st century, there has been a significant rise in the number of Americans claiming Indigenous heritage. Analysts say that the trend is not attributable to birth rates or immigration, but instead reflects the growing number of Americans wishing to formally claim their Native identities.

Native people in the United States have suffered centuries of violence, displacement and forced assimilation that began with the arrival of European colonists in the 1600s. During the eighteenth and nineteenth centuries, Native people were subjected to countless broken treaties and government policies designed to strip them of their land, sovereignty and culture. The Indian Removal Act of 1830 forced Cherokee Indians to march westward from their ancestral lands along a brutal and often deadly route known as the Trail of Tears.

Over time, reservations were carved up and forcibly sold, dances and ceremonies were outlawed and Native children were forced into English-only boarding schools. The legacy of dispossession is not over. Today, Native languages are in decline, with many already extinct, or spoken by only a handful of elders. Racism and poverty, particularly in America's inner cities, make it even harder for Native communities to preserve their traditional ways of life.

Promisingly, the Biden-Harris administration invested billions in Native American interests and today Native communities are mobilizing to preserve their culture, holding festivals and Powwows. The Cherokee Nation has implemented in-school and online Native language lessons, while in Montana, members of the Blackfeet Nation are managing tribal land as their ancestors did to reintroduce free-roaming bison after a 150-year absence.

**Location:**
Various regions of the US, especially the Southwest (Navajo Nation, Arizona, New Mexico) and the Great Plains (South Dakota, North Dakota)

**Threat:**
Dispossession

# Uncontacted: Brazil's rainforest communities

**Location:**
Javari Valley, western Amazon rainforest, Brazil

**Threat:**
Illegal mining and logging; drug trafficking

The Amazonian rainforest, hostile to most outsiders, provides the Indigenous people of Brazil's Javari Valley with everything they need: food, shelter, medicine and the means to enjoy family life.

The valley is located in Brazil's far west, near the borders with Peru and Colombia. An immense area of rugged terrain, roughly the size of Portugal, it's reachable only by snaking brown-water rivers and is home to one of the largest concentrations of uncontacted Indigenous communities on earth. It's hardly surprising that the valley's uncontacted groups typically avoid contact with outsiders. Illegal mining, logging, fishing and hunting, as well as disease brought by outsiders, have all had a devastating impact on their health and quality of life.

The hidden waterways of the Javari valley have become a major drug trafficking route in recent years. Local communities are caught in the battleground between Colombian and Brazilian cartels who fight for control of the water. Indigenous teens are recruited to drug gangs and murder rates have soared to the point that Javari Valley now belongs to Brazil's most violent state. In 2022, British journalist Dom Phillips and Brazilian Indigenous expert Bruno Pereira were killed in the Javari Valley by men linked to organized crime.

The situation worsened when former president Jair Bolsonaro relaxed environmental protections, which led to surges in deforestation and other illegal activity in the valley. Hopes were reignited by the 2023 election of President Luiz Inácio Lula da Silva, whose administration created the first Ministry of Native People to advance and protect the interests of Indigenous people. Even with legal protections, Brazil's uncontacted groups remain vulnerable. Despite choosing to live in isolation, communities endure a barrage of external pressures that threaten their ancestral land, way of life and even their personal safety.

# Hair today, gone tomorrow: Failure to freeze in Yukon, Canada

**Location:**
Eclipse Nordic Hot Springs, near Whitehorse, southern Yukon territory, Canada

**Threat:**
Climate change

VANISHING CULTURAL PRACTICE

When temperatures plunge to -20°C, most people crave only blankets and a cosy fire. For residents of Whitehorse, in Canada's Yukon Territory, however, it signals the start of their annual hair freezing competition.

The contest, which began in 2011, invites gutsy participants to turn their hair into outlandish icy sculptures and compete for cash. How does it work? Contestants plunge into a natural hot spring, submerging their heads in the 40°C water. Then, while keeping their bodies in the water, but exposing their heads and shoulders, they allow the cold air to gradually freeze their hair, including their eyelashes, eyebrows and beards. Participants shape their freezing hair into weird and wonderful designs and, once their hair is pure white with ice and rigid, they ring the bell so a photograph can be taken for the judges.

Efforts are judged according to six categories: best male, best female, best group, most creative, best facial hair and people's choice. The winner of each scoops $2,000 (£1,600). The competition is held any time between December and March, as soon as the temperature drops below -20°C, the minimum chill required for hair to freeze. Sadly though, both the 2023/24 and 2024/25 events had to be cancelled because temperatures failed to drop low enough. Neither winter came close to being cold enough to sustain a frozen hairdo.

A 2022 report from Yukon University states that climate change is causing warmer winters in the region and predicts that winters could continue to warm by 3.7°C over the next 50 years. Though lighthearted in spirit, Yukon's hair freezing competition has become part of the local cultural fabric. Now, rising global temperatures have cast a chilling shadow over the future of this eccentric tradition, threatening to thaw the bond between people and place.

# End of the road? Alaska's buckling highway

**Location:**
Dalton Highway, from Fairbanks to Deadhorse, northern Alaska, USA

**Threat:**
Climate change

Slicing through the Alaskan wilderness, the Dalton Highway is a solitary road through a vast frozen landscape. Its northernmost stretch passes through a tundra shaped by frost, where trees cannot grow. On polar nights, this snowy land is cloaked in darkness, lit only by the low Arctic sun and the dance of the Northern Lights.

The Dalton is not for the faint-hearted. Traffic along its 666 kilometres is made up of hunters, researchers, and tourists chasing auroras and adventure. Its lifeblood though, is truckers. Every day, around 200 18-wheel rigs thunder up the highway, hauling 2,500 tons of fuel and vital supplies northward to Prudhoe Bay and remote Arctic communities. The Dalton was built in 1974 to support the Trans-Alaska Pipeline, connecting Fairbanks in Alaska to the Arctic Ocean. It's the only road to and from the Arctic Circle and a lifeline for isolated communities.

The Alaskan icon is cracking under the weight of a changing climate. The road is built on permafrost, which thaws in rising temperatures, causing it to sink and buckle. Colossal underground landslides threaten to damage the highway, and intense flooding, driven by snowmelt and heavy rains, has washed out entire sections. At times, the Dalton becomes a dangerous obstacle course for truckers. Maintenance crews are locked in a perpetual race against nature.

Flooding and permafrost have intensified in recent decades and in 2015, catastrophic flooding closed the road for several weeks. Millions have been spent to elevate and reinforce the Dalton, and reroute its fragile sections. Some experts question whether maintenance crews can ever catch up but, despite doubt and mounting costs, hope persists. Innovative engineering and decent funding, bolstered by Alaskan resolve, could pave the way to survival.

# Lights out? Puerto Rico's bioluminescent bays

As night settles over the still bay at La Parguera, in southwestern Puerto Rico, an extraordinary phenomenon unfolds. The water is home to millions of microscopic plankton called dinoflagellates, which emit bursts of fluorescent blue light when they are disturbed by fish or kayaks. Like minuscule underwater fireflies, they flicker and swirl, illuminating the darkness with an otherworldly glow.

**Location:**
La Parguera Bioluminescent Bay, Lajas, southwestern Puerto Rico

**Threat:**
Development

This natural spectacle, known as bioluminescence, has long attracted tourists, who bring a welcome boost to the local economy. Lately though, a wave of wealthy newcomers, many seeking second homes in the bay, has fuelled a surge in development. Luxury resorts and waterfront mansions encroach on the shoreline, while jet skis rip through once-tranquil waters, disrupting the community and the bay's fragile ecosystem.

Residents protest against unchecked development and demand implementation of stricter environmental regulations, while tour companies attempt to minimize their environmental impact by using electric boats. A community leader in La Parguera is fighting to ban bright Christmas lights on houseboats, which he warns could damage the ecological balance of the bay.

Conservation efforts have succeeded elsewhere. A decade ago, the brightest and most famous of Puerto Rico's three bioluminescent bays, Mosquito Bay, started to dim. Strict restrictions were quickly enforced, limiting construction, banning motorboats and prohibiting swimming in the bay. In time, the dinoflagellates recovered and Mosquito Bay once again pulsated with light. With a renewed focus on conservation and responsible tourism, there's every reason to believe La Parguera's water will shine for years to come.

# Exodus: Panama's evacuated island

**Location:**
Gardi Sugdub island, Guna Yala territory, Caribbean coast of Panama

**Threat:**
Climate change

In the spring of 2024 around 300 families packed up their belongings and left the island that they and their ancestors had inhabited for centuries. They had no choice – the land could soon be underwater.

When the Guna community evacuated from Gardi Sugdub island, in the San Blas archipelago off Panama's Caribbean coast, they became among the first climate refugees in the Americas. Gardi Sugdub is roughly the size of five football pitches and its highest point is just one metre above sea level. In the years leading up to the evacuation, the island's narrow dusty streets regularly flooded at high tide. Rising sea levels and overcrowding eventually made life on the island simply unsustainable and unsafe.

Residents collaborated with the Panamanian government to create a new home for their community on the mainland. The move to the Isber Yala town meant swapping ocean-facing reed and zinc-roofed huts for prefabricated concrete buildings, a few kilometres inland from the coast. While this was the first case in Central America of a planned mass-evacuation of an island due to climate change, it almost certainly won't be the last. Panama's Ministry of Environment warns that much of the San Blas archipelago will be uninhabitable by 2050. With NASA predicting that global sea levels could rise by more than a metre if emissions aren't reduced, mass-relocations could be repeated across the world.

The Guna people's cultural identity is deeply tied to the ocean. Moving inland has disrupted their traditional way of life and fostered a greater reliance on canned supermarket food. The relocation to Isber Yala has been bittersweet for the community. In their new mainland town, Guna families have more space and a more secure future, but they face the trauma of watching from a distance as their ancestral home is swallowed by the sea.

# Engulfed: Los Angeles County's scorched landscape

**Location:**
Los Angeles County, Southern California, USA

**Threat:**
Wildfires

In 2025, Los Angeles County experienced some of the most catastrophic wildfires in its history. Starting on 7th January, a series of blazes ripped across the region, propelled by a perfect storm of tinder-dry vegetation and hurricane-force Santa Ana winds. By month's end, when the fires were finally contained, over 15,000 hectares lay in smoldering ruin.

Among the largest of these infernos, the Palisades Fire, left a trail of devastation across Pacific Palisades, Topanga and Malibu. A landscape once famed for hiking trails, cliffside houses and beachfront mansions was transformed into a blackened wasteland. Heartbroken families watched as the fire devoured 9,489 hectares, reducing their homes to ash.

Simultaneously, the Eaton Fire scorched 5,674 hectares of the San Gabriel foothills. Altadena, a historic haven for Black artistry and activism, was hit especially hard. Nearly half of its Black-owned homes were destroyed, in a devastating blow to the area's unique cultural heritage.

The wildfires left deep scars, not least financial. With damages projected to surpass £200 billion, they are estimated to be the costliest natural disaster in United States history. Amidst the wreckage, the community rallied. Evacuation centres were flooded with donations, distributed by an army of volunteers.

The catastrophe prompted some residents to leave the fire-prone state – a pattern that demographic experts foresee becoming increasingly common. While investigators search for the cause of the wildfires, theories circulate. Fingers have been pointed at arsonists, hikers, utility companies and re-ignited embers from a previous fire. As the people of LA County rebuild, the tourism board issues a simple message to tourists: We're counting on you.

# Show's over: The half-built National Art Schools of Cuba

**Location:**
National Art Schools, former Country Club of Havana grounds, western Cuba

**Threat:**
Neglect

Cuba's National Art Schools, in Havana's leafy outskirts, are an echo of post-revolutionary ambition. The project was born in 1961, during a round of golf between Fidel Castro and Che Guevara. Over mojitos at the Havana Country Club, the friends envisioned building a utopian arts school where they stood; a campus to symbolise Cuba's cultural future, and nurture post-revolution creativity.

Castro chose Cuban modernist architect Ricardo Porro and Italians Roberto Gottardi and Vittorio Garatti to design a campus with five schools for ballet, music, plastic arts, dramatic arts, and modern dance. Their revolutionary designs used local materials like red bricks and terracotta tiles, with fluid, open spaces to inspire creativity. The ballet school featured domed roofs and arched walkways, while the music school's spiralling structure evoked musical notes.

Construction kicked off quickly but, like so many utopian dreams, it was derailed by changing political currents. As Soviet influence took hold in Cuba, its Ministry of Building Works began to favour functionalist form over the experimental design of the campus. By the mid-1960s, the Cuban government deemed the National Arts Schools impractical and extravagant, and withdrew funding.

In 2000, the half-built campus, now decaying and veiled in vegetation, was added to the World Monuments Fund's endangered list. Its recognition by the heritage organisation led to renewed interest, and it was made a Cuban National Monument in 2011. Intermittent restoration attempts followed, with some buildings rehabilitated for students and exhibitions. In 2020, the Getty Foundation funded the creation of a comprehensive preservation plan for the campus, but it is yet to be implemented. Castro and Guevara's golf course dream, though incomplete, refuses to fade.

# Crack in the road: Honduras's nefarious narco-highway

**Location:**
Río Plátano Biosphere Reserve, Mosquitia region, northeastern Honduras

**Threat:**
Illegal activity

In the remote La Moskitia region of northeastern Honduras, the Río Plátano Biosphere Reserve is one of the most impressive ecosystems on the planet. Rivers carve wide arches through forests that are home to endangered species like giant anteaters, Mexican spider monkeys, and great green macaws. The Reserve is a UNESCO World Heritage Site and one of Central America's last tropical rainforests.

Yet, deforestation has surged, driven by illegal invasions by cattle ranchers, loggers, mineral miners and drug traffickers, who operate under the cover of the rainforest. Exotic animals are poached for the illegal pet trade, while Indigenous communities face threats of violence, land loss, and forced displacement.

In 2021, it became widely known that a major illegal road had been built through the Reserve, pushing far into Indigenous territories. The so-called narco-highway is likely used for smuggling drugs, timber and other contraband. As well as causing ecological devastation and political turmoil, the unlawful road threatens the rights and livelihoods of Indigenous populations.

Indigenous leaders have said that, of all threats facing the Río Plátano, this road is the greatest. They have accused the Honduran government of turning a blind eye, warning that politicians are in the pockets of drug cartels. Despite repeated pleas, the road remains open, with no official guards or patrols to protect the Reserve from criminals.

In May 2024, the Honduran government launched Zero Deforestation by 2029, a plan to reclaim protected areas and dismantle illegal operations using military force. However, there is skepticism about whether this will be enough to counteract years of systemic corruption and criminal control. The vibrant Honduran rainforest could become a beacon for ecotourism, but only once the government takes down the criminals who threaten its survival.

# Groundbreaking: Florida's sinkholes

**Location:**
Sinkhole Alley: Pasco County, Hernando County and Hillsborough County, central Florida, USA

**Threat:**
Ground collapse

Nicknamed Disney for Seniors, The Villages is a sprawling retirement community in Florida. Residents enjoy a life of sunshine and security, but a surreal threat looms large. The Villages neighbours an area of Florida nicknamed Sinkhole Alley, where the phenomenon occurs more frequently than anywhere else in the United States.

Notoriously unpredictable, sinkholes form when water dissolves soluble underground rock, eventually causing the ground above to collapse. Florida's porous limestone bedrock makes it a sinkhole hotspot. The most common type is a gradual sinking, with creaking walls, sagging fences and titling floors acting as early warning signs. The other, less common and more terrifying type, is known as cover collapse, occurring when the ground suddenly gives way without warning.

Sinkhole casualties are rare. The majority happen gradually and are little more than a costly headache for residents. A cover collapse, however, can be catastrophic. In 2013, Jeffrey Bush of Seffner, Florida, was swallowed by a sinkhole in his sleep. After Hurricane Milton in 2024, a wave of giant chasms opened up across West-Central Florida, some devouring entire buildings. Research scientists propose that rapid development in Sinkhole Alley has accelerated sinkhole formation, as roads, buildings and modified drainage systems have put increasing pressure on Florida's fragile underground terrain.

For those living with the lingering fear of the ground giving way beneath them, technology offers some reassurance. Ground-penetrating radar and other geophysical tools are used to detect potential collapses. Sinkholes are natural, but careful urban planning and monitoring can reduce the risks and help the Villages' residents sleep more soundly.

# Beaten track: South America's overgrown Incan roads

**Location:**
Andean Road System, spanning Argentina, Bolivia, Chile, Colombia, Ecuador and Peru

**Threat:**
Development and environmental degradation

Built by the Incas and their predecessors, the Andean Road System, or Qhapaq Ñan, is a remarkable road network that spans over 30,000 kilometres. It connected six modern-day South American countries, providing the empire's diverse settlements and ethnic groups with a cohesive system for trade, communication and defense.

A UNESCO World Heritage site, the road system is celebrated as one of humanity's most impressive feats of engineering. Its trails stretch from the snow-capped mountains of the Andes, to sweltering rainforests, via valleys and deserts. Llamas and alpacas once transported goods along its pathways of cobblestone and compacted earth, while the empire's swift-footed runners carried messages great distances across the most extreme terrains on earth.

The route – equivalent to crossing the United States at its widest point seven times – is dotted with fortresses, agricultural terraces and other historic, archaeological sites, 273 of which are components of the UNESCO status. Its most famous segment, leading to Machu Picchu, has come to be known as the Inca Trail and is trekked by hundreds of tourists each day.

While sections of the network are preserved, much has deteriorated since the Spanish conquest. Overgrown with vegetation and disrupted by modern infrastructure and shifting weather patterns, large sections have been lost.

An increase in tourism along parts of the road brings economic opportunities, but must be carefully managed to protect cultural heritage and local communities. The World Monuments Fund added the Andean road system to its 2025 watchlist, advocating for sustainable tourism and careful, collaborative stewardship that respects the people who live alongside it.

# Port of no return? Venezuela's town in turmoil

**Location:**
Coro and its port, La Vela de Coro, Falcón State, northwestern Venezuela

**Threat:**
Neglect

Coro, a historic town on Venezuela's northwest coast, is lined with earthen buildings painted in warm peach and yellow tones, blending Caribbean, Spanish and Indigenous architectural styles. Founded in 1527 as Venezuela's first capital, Coro played a central role during Spanish colonization. Its cathedral still bears gun holes from pirate raids in the 1500s. The town's port of La Vela stands as a symbol of independence, said to be the first South American town to achieve freedom from Spain.

For twenty years, Coro and its port have been on UNESCO's World Heritage in Danger list, crumbling under the weight of Venezuela's political and economic collapse. Extreme rainfall, poor drainage and neglect accelerate the town's decline. Some homes have fallen down, while others are held up with makeshift wooden props or covered in plastic tarps. Successive governors have pledged restoration, yet little has been done. Corruption has siphoned millions of dollars earmarked for repairs.

Daily life for Venezuelans is a struggle. Food shortages and mind-boggling rates of hyperinflation (at times exceeding one million percent) force residents in smaller towns to resort to bartering, swapping vegetables for car repairs. Public services like running water, electricity and mobile phone networks are not guaranteed. Concerned about safety, international governments advise against travel. In a country fighting for survival, there is little room for historical conservation.

Restoring Coro requires solutions that feel out of reach, starting with political and economic stability. Rejoining the global economy could bring tourism and investment, allowing for the specialised restoration work that UNESCO recommends. The people of Coro and La Vela struggle on, waiting for a long-promised revival.

BLOCKBUSTER
211
DROP BOX
179·XVE
COLORADO
HIGHLANDER

# 'Til the bitter end: The last Blockbuster on Earth

**Location:**
Blockbuster, Revere Avenue, Bend, central Oregon, USA

**Threat:**
Modernization

In the outdoorsy city of Bend, Oregon, people can ski in the morning, kayak in the afternoon and play golf as the sun sets. Or, for an adventure of a different kind, they can visit the last Blockbuster store on earth.

In defiance of streaming trends, Bend's Blockbuster store sells and rents video cassettes, DVDs, Blu-rays and video games. The once prolific blue and gold signage above the door is just the start of the nostalgia-fest for millennial film fans, with locals and tourists flocking to relive the video rental experience of their youth. While new releases are available, classic films remain the most popular.

Once a global chain, Blockbuster dominated the video rental industry in the late 1990s and early 2000s, with 9,000 stores in the United States alone. However, the arrival of Netflix and other on-demand digital services toppled the empire and, by 2010, Blockbuster was bankrupt. Stores began to close and the business was bought by US TV provider Dish Network, which licensed the name to franchise holders. A few Blockbusters endured in Alaska, where unreliable internet gave them an advantage, and in Australia, but the last of these closed in 2019, leaving Bend the only store standing.

The store's managers capitalize on its unique status by selling merchandise. They even published an apocalyptic-themed Instagram advert during the Super Bowl, which went viral. The advert proclaimed that, when the world ends and streaming services are no more, Blockbuster in Bend will still be here. It ended with the store's slogan: 'Til the bitter end.

Despite rumours of its demise, Bend's Blockbuster lives on. What happens, though, when the nostalgia-driven crowd eventually dwindles? Will the last Blockbuster on earth bow out like thousands before it, or truly fight on 'til the bitter end?

# Africa

# The sands of time: The Namibian town swallowed by desert

**Location:**
Kolmanskop, near the coastal town of Lüderitz, southern Namibia

**Threat:**
Encroaching desert sands

It's said that, in Kolmanskop's heyday, people would crawl through town on their hands and knees, filling jam jars with the diamonds they scooped easily from the sand.

Diamonds were discovered in the remote Namibian settlement by a railway worker in 1908. Before then, the area was little more than a barren desert outpost, used mainly as a stopover for miners. After the discovery, the authorities declared the region a restricted mining zone and a frenzied diamond rush ensued. The town evolved into a prosperous community, home to several hundred Namibian and European miners. As well as a casino, a ballroom and an ice factory, the town had a hospital that boasted the first X-ray machine in the southern hemisphere. At its peak, in 1912, Kolmanskop produced one million carats of diamonds, nearly twelve percent of the world's total.

Sometimes though, diamonds are not forever. Mining was temporarily halted by World War I and subsequently, when richer diamond deposits were found elsewhere, people moved on. The last residents left Kolmanskop in the 1950s, leaving it to the whims of the desert.

Since then, the town's empty buildings have been battered by nature. Windows and doors have blown in, ceilings have collapsed and sand has swept in, piling up in every room and building. The sand is so high inside some houses that visitors have to lie on their stomachs to squeeze through doorways.

Diamond mining in the region has mostly moved south and off shore. The restricted zone around Kolmanskop is still in place but, with the correct permit, curious tourists and photographers can explore. It's hard to believe that, less than 100 years ago, this deserted and derelict town was among the wealthiest in the world. Now, it's only a matter of time before Kolmanskop is entirely reclaimed by nature.

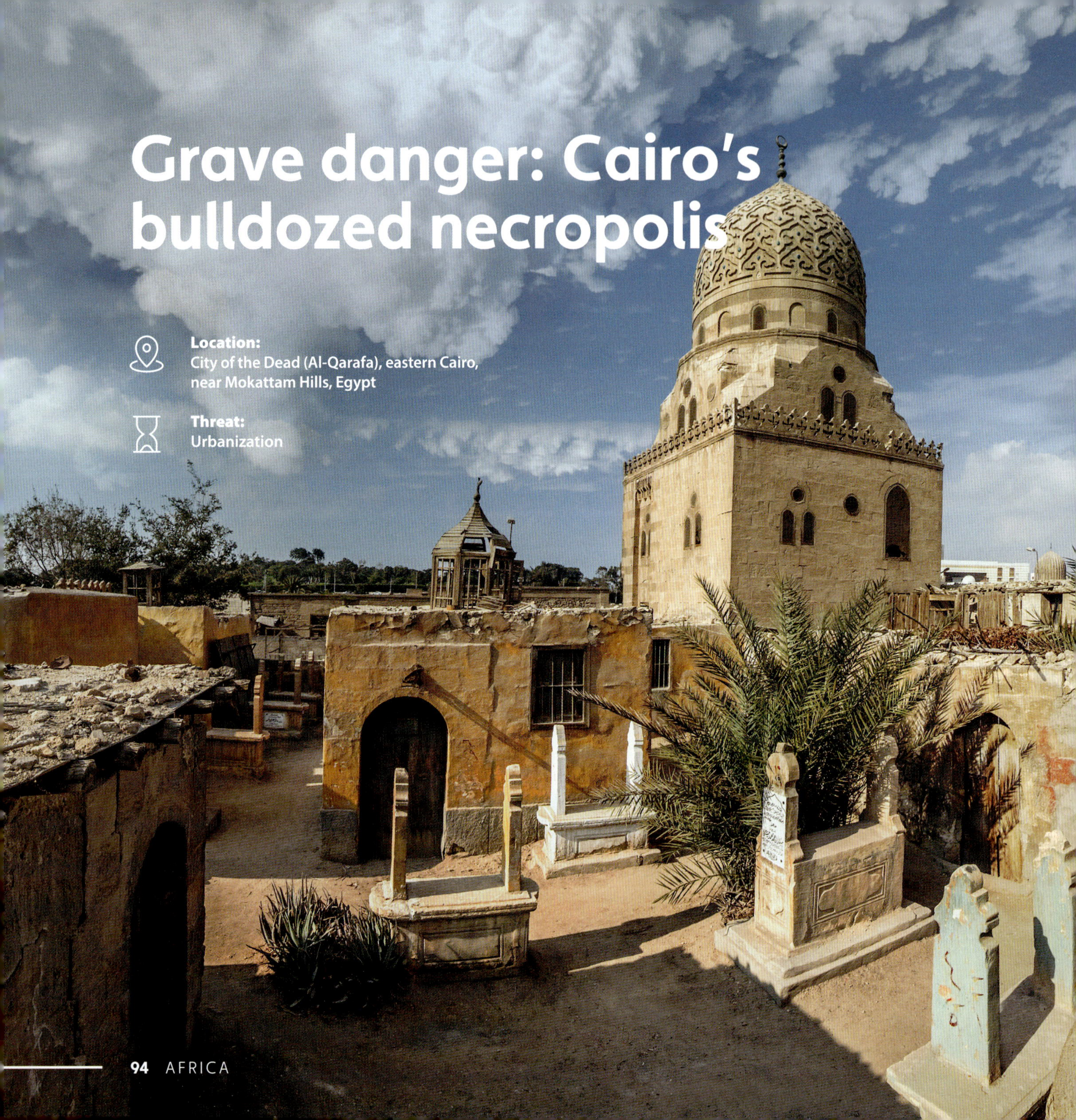

# Grave danger: Cairo's bulldozed necropolis

**Location:**
City of the Dead (Al-Qarafa), eastern Cairo, near Mokattam Hills, Egypt

**Threat:**
Urbanization

From revolutionaries to kings, countless influential figures from Cairo's history have been laid to rest in the City of the Dead. This iconic burial ground dates back to the seventh century. Its cobblestone streets are lined with grand mosques and mausoleums that have witnessed the rise and fall of kingdoms. Over thousands of years, the graveyard has expanded to fill six square kilometres (the size of 840 football pitches) and now belongs to a UNESCO World Heritage Site area known as Historic Cairo.

In 2020, government-authorized bulldozers rolled into the necropolis and began uprooting and relocating graves, to make way for a road. The City's governor then banned burials in certain areas, earmarked for demolition. Many historical mausoleums have since been torn down, and ancient graves relocated. In 2023, the government even asked UNESCO to reduce the borders of Historic Cairo. UNESCO denied the request and instead expressed concern.

The government's ongoing prioritization of urban development over the preservation of cultural heritage has sparked outcry, not least from the families of the buried. Concerns are mounting about the decimation of a place of profound cultural and spiritual significance. Since 2019, volunteers have been racing to document graves and salvage what artefacts they can for museums.

The government argues demolition is necessary to modernize Cairo's Islamic quarter, ease congestion and create public parks. In 2023, the Prime Minister announced that 20,000 graves had been built on the outskirts of Cairo for relocated tombs. The new cemetery even contains a special area for deceased Egyptian celebrities, called the Graves of the Glorious. Locals remain sceptical. The push of Cairo's urbanization feels unrelenting; they worry even the dead cannot escape it.

# Paradise lost: The Kenyan hotel lost to the ocean

**Location:**
Kipini Village, Tana River County, Kenya, where the mouth of the Tana River meets the Indian Ocean

**Threat:**
Deforestation and climate change

The quiet fishing village of Kipini, on the northernmost tip of Kenya's Tana River County, was once a favorite holiday spot for Kenyan government officials and travellers seeking undiscovered places. At its centre was the Tana Lodge Hotel, built in the mid-1990s, atop sand dunes one hundred metres from the shore of the Indian Ocean.

For a time, the hotel flourished, drawing visitors from across the world who cherished its unspoiled seclusion. However, rising sea levels have gradually shattered life in Kipini. According to a local administrator, nearly ten kilometres of land has been lost to the sea in the last ten years. By 2023, the Tana Lodge Hotel had been largely washed away, leaving dozens of workers unemployed and the local tourism industry in tatters.

The problem is linked to the loss of mangrove forests along the shoreline. They are the coast's main defense against erosion, but they have been depleted by deforestation and the effects of climate change, leaving the village exposed. Groundwater has turned saline, spoiling fresh water supplies and making farming impossible. Fearing their homes, further inland, will meet the same fate as the hotel, a growing number of residents are relocating.

Some locals say the rising sea levels are caused by the Tana River changing course, but scientists lay the blame squarely at the feet of climate change. Local authorities have proposed building a sea wall along the coastline, once funds are raised, while climate experts stress the need to restore the mangrove forests. The owner of Tana Lodge, Mr Macri, has moved to another town. There is nothing for him in Kipini now that his beloved hotel has succumbed to the sea.

# Kingdom of clay: Ghana's last ten Asante houses

**Location:**
Villages north and northeast of Kumasi, central Ghana

**Threat:**
Neglect

Asante was once one of the most powerful states on the African continent, but most of the architecture Indigenous to the eighteenth and nineteenth century kingdom has been lost to time. In fact, only ten traditional Asante buildings are believed to remain.

The surviving buildings are all shrine houses made from timber, bamboo and mud, and would once have had thatched roofs. Images of crocodiles, fish and birds are interwoven with a proliferation of plant imagery in the elaborate murals and modelling that adorn the structures. These designs had rich symbolic meaning that would have been understood perfectly by the Asante people of the time. Asante culture is known for non-verbal communication; symbols could express almost all activities. A common motif is of the Sankofa bird standing with its head turned backward – a reminder to refer to one's past, as a guide to the future.

The earthen shrines must contend with natural deterioration and central Ghana's unforgiving tropical climate. Historically, they would have been maintained by master craftsmen from each village, but the twentieth century saw traditional methods displaced by some more cost-effective processes using modern materials like corrugated iron roofing and cement plaster.

Since 1980, the buildings have been on the UNESCO World Heritage List of protected properties, but a plan for longterm upkeep and stewardship of the shrines is still wanting. As the last surviving examples of this style of Asante architecture, the ten houses need more than sporadic emergency interventions. According to the United States' heritage organisation, the World Monuments Fund, the key to their long-term survival is community stewardship and local people mastering traditional Asante skills.

# Final chapter? Mauritania's disappearing libraries

**Location:**
Chinguetti, Sahara Desert, western Mauritania, Northwest Africa

**Threat:**
Desertification

Deep in the Sahara desert, in the oasis city of Chinguetti, a handful of weathered libraries house manuscripts that are centuries-old. The twelfth-century city was once a busy trade and religious centre along the trans-Saharan trade route. Pilgrims and traders brought manuscripts from elsewhere in the Islamic world, containing knowledge on astronomy, science, theology and poetry.

The texts, collected over centuries and passed through generations, are stored in family-owned libraries. There were once 30 such libraries in Chinguetti but, in the 1930s, families began leaving to find pasture for camels and jobs, taking their books with them. Now, only twelve libraries remain and protecting them is becoming increasingly difficult.

Manuscripts, some written on fragile gazelle skin, are at risk from wind, rain, sand and of course, heat. Pages are nibbled by termites and goats. With no air conditioning in the dry-stone wall buildings, desperate librarians place buckets of water near bookshelves to lower the room temperature. As the desert expands, more sand encroaches on Chinguetti every year, threatening to engulf the libraries. Some are already close to being buried, and librarians have to dig sand away from the doors to open them.

Select manuscripts are being digitized, though the work is delicate and slow. Preservationists call for the books to be relocated for safety, but locals resist, asking instead for support to preserve the books within the city. Talking to the BBC in 2020, librarian Saif al Islam al Ahmed Mahmoud warned that the manuscripts cannot survive away from the libraries. "It is impossible to give up your house, your leg or your eye and preserve them at the same time", he said. "This is our inheritance."

# Mountains of the Moon: Uganda's thawing ice

**Location:**
Rwenzori Mountains, Uganda-Democratic Republic of Congo border, East Africa

**Threat:**
Climate change

The Bakonzo people, Indigenous to the Rwenzori mountains, revere the glaciers that crown these peaks as the dwelling place of their god. The community holds ceremonies at sacred sites throughout the mountain range, which straddles the border between Uganda and the Democratic Republic of the Congo. They offer prayers for their harvests, and use water from glacial streams for baptisms and healing rituals.

The glaciers also provide an income for Rwenzori trekking guides and contribute to a water supply on which many families, farmers and fishermen depend. For scientists, they hold data about the largely undocumented climate history of equatorial Africa. The glaciers are a critical part of the alpine ecosystem which, if disrupted, could drive rare plant and animal species to extinction.

Photos taken in 1906 of the Stanley Glacier, tucked between the two highest peaks of Mount Stanley, show a thick covering of ice across the top of the range. Today, the ice covers less than one square kilometre. Glaciers in the Rwenzori range, nicknamed the Mountains of the Moon, have diminished by around 67 percent since 2005. If current climate trends persist, some researchers predict the glaciers may vanish within decades.

In 2023, the World Wide Fund for Nature (WWF) and its partners launched a five-year project called Restoration for a Resilient Rwenzori. It focuses on restoring landscapes, building environmental resilience and empowering alpine communities against climate change. The WWF also collaborates with local organisations to train communities to sustainably manage their natural resources.

Conservationists and communities are dedicated to halting the glaciers' recession and preserving the ecosystems and livelihoods that depend on them. Without global action on climate change, though, this may not be enough.

# Plundered past: Sudan's stolen riches

**Location:**
Meroë Pyramids, Nile Valley, northern Sudan

**Threat:**
Civil war

It sounds almost farcical: priceless historical treasures stolen from war-ravaged Sudan, turning up for sale on eBay. The listings featured paintings, pottery, and gold artifacts, which were swiftly removed after British newspaper *The Times* alerted the auction site. While the items had been described by the eBay seller as Egyptian antiques, experts suspect they were actually plundered from Sudan's National Museum in Khartoum.

The museum, among the most important in Africa, houses artefacts from the Palaeolithic, Meroë, Christian, and Islamic eras, including figurines used in the burials of Kushite kings. When civil war broke out between the Rapid Support Forces (RSF) and the Sudanese Armed Forces (SAF) in April 2023, the museum was in the process of being renovated. Many exhibits were packed into storage boxes, making any would-be looter's job easier.

Sudan's national broadcaster reported large-scale looting of the museum carried out by RSF soldiers, though the RSF denies involvement. The ancient pyramids of Meroë, an iconic symbol of Sudan, are also believed to be in danger. Rising from the desert between the Nile and Atbara rivers, Meroë's pyramids have stood for over 2,500 years as a legacy of the ancient Kingdom of Kush, which once rivaled Egypt in power and artistry. As RSF forces draw closer, fears grow that plundering and destruction will follow.

Reports of looting have become so persistent that, in September 2024, UNESCO announced that the threat to Sudan's culture had reached unprecedented levels. The art-buying community was warned not to purchase Sudanese cultural property, as illegal trade risks erasing the country's cultural identity. Heritage bodies like UNESCO and individual caretakers strive to protect Sudan's historical legacy, but they face a formidable challenge.

# Benin's battered icon: The Great Mosque

**Location:**
Great Mosque, Porto-Novo, southern Benin, West Africa

**Threat:**
Neglect

In the centre of Benin's historic capital, Porto-Novo, stands the Great Mosque, its weary facade defying its name. Large sections of the building's vaulted ceiling have collapsed, its towers are crumbling and trees grow through cracks in its walls.

Built between 1912 and 1925, the once-mighty mosque embodies the identity of the Aguda people who constructed it. They are descendants of Afro-Brazilians who returned to West Africa in the nineteenth century after emancipation. Craftsmanship was a means of reclaiming power in the face of discrimination and, drawing on Brazilian and Portuguese influences, the community sought to create buildings of high status to forge themselves a new identity. Architectural triumphs, including the Great Mosque, wove Aguda heritage into the fabric of Benin.

As a developing country, Benin has limited resources for specialist maintenance and restoration, and the mosque has succumbed to time. However, historians and technology experts from universities in Benin and the United States have collaborated to ensure its legacy survives, even as its physical form fades. In 2023, they launched the African Building Heritage Project, using drone scans, VR, and photography to preserve a digital version of Benin's mosque in an easily accessible archive.

The project also aims to capture the stories and spirit of the people who built and worshipped in the mosque. Researchers interviewed community members and stakeholders to understand the building's place in local lives and culture. Porto-Novo's Great Mosque may one day fall to ruin, but digital preservation allows it to remain part of Benin's story. The team hopes their project will serve as a digital blueprint for preserving more at-risk buildings across West Africa.

# Stonewalled: South Africa's overlooked ruins

**Location:**
Blaauboschkraal stone ruins, Mpumalanga province, northeastern South Africa

**Threat:**
Neglect

In the Mpumalanga province of South Africa lies a sprawling complex of stone walls, terraces and circular homesteads known as the Blaauboschkraal stone ruins. Mystery surrounds them, but the structures are widely believed to have been built in the early sixteenth century by the Bokoni people, a pre-colonial agricultural society.

The Bokoni were skilled farmers and traders, who likely exchanged crops for metals and ivory. The ruins are thought to have served multiple purposes, including cattle enclosures, agricultural terracing and housing. The circular homestead layout is a defining feature of Bokoni settlements. By the 1830s, however, conflict had driven the Bokoni people from the region, and their once-thriving settlements were abandoned.

Neglect and erosion from wind and rain threaten the fragile remains and the stone walls are crumbling. Although the ruins are a recognised provincial heritage site, they lack the comprehensive protections given to South Africa's more famous locations, such as the legendary fossil site in Gauteng, the Cradle of Humankind. This lack of attention has left unanswered questions, giving rise to alternative theories. South African politician Michael Tellinger – often dismissed as fuelling conspiracy theories – claims the site is an ancient astronomical calendar built by aliens 300,000 years ago, to align with Orion's Belt. While historians disagree, the ruins' full story remains buried.

Historians and archaeologists urge leaders in the Mpumalanga province to do more to maintain the integrity of the Blaauboschkraal site, calling for a comprehensive audit of the stones and a crack down on vandalism. With proper protection, the mysterious ruins could be preserved as lasting monuments to the Bokoni people's untold history.

# Changing currents: Zambia's faltering floodplain

In Western Zambia, the Zambezi River carves through a vast plain, creating a landscape like no other. Stretching 10,750 square kilometres at peak flooding, the Barotse Floodplain is an expanse of grasslands, forests and waterways, shaped by the rhythm of floods. For centuries, the Lozi people have lived in harmony with the Zambezi, adapting in ingenious ways to its seasonal rise and fall.

During the dry season, the floodplain buzzes with life, as the Lozi people farm, graze cattle, and fish the abundant waters. When the rains come, the river swells, transforming the plain into a huge inland sea. Peak flooding, around April, is the community's call to relocate to higher ground.

Their annual migration culminates with the Kuomboka ceremony, meaning "emerging from the waters". The Litunga (Lozi king) is ferried to higher ground on the royal Nalikwanda barge, painted in black-and-white zebra stripes and adorned with the emblem of a leaping elephant. The king leads a jubilant procession through the labyrinth of canals, accompanied by pounding drums and singing. Families follow in their canoes, cattle in tow, to seek refuge for around four months on man-made mounds that rise like islands from the floodplain.

However, climate change has thrown the river's once-predictable rhythms into chaos. Longer droughts, sudden floods and erratic seasons disrupt farming and fishing. Meanwhile, silt and decaying plants clog the canals, while planned infrastructure like roads and hydropower projects threaten the community's way of life. In 2025, the World Monuments Fund added the floodplain to its watchlist, highlighting the need to protect it. A month later, the Zambian government nominated it for UNESCO World Heritage status, a designation that could lead to much-needed conservation funding and sustainable tourism.

**Location:**
Barotse Floodplain, along the Zambezi River, Western Province, Zambia, Southern Africa

**Threat:**
Development and climate change

# Coming soon? Angola's unfinished modernist cinema

**Location:**
Cinema Studio Namibe, Moçâmedes, southwestern Angola

**Threat:**
Neglect

A structure likened to a spaceship, a mushroom, or even the twisted, leathery Welwitchia plant of the Namib desert, Cinema Studio Namibe in the port city of Moçâmedes is a movie theatre that's never shown a film.

Angola experienced a surge in cinema construction between the 1940s and early 1970s, aligning with the peak of the modernist architectural movement. The cinemas were initially created as propaganda tools by the Portuguese colonial regime, but they quickly became popular social spaces.

In 1973, construction began on a new cinema for Moçâmedes, designed by Portuguese architect, Botelho Vasconcelos. One of the finest examples of tropical modernist architecture in Angola, Cinema Studio Namibe adapts progressive modernist principles to the country's climate. The structure was built using exposed reinforced concrete, with a semi-enclosed dome to filter sunlight and provide ventilation. The building's sandy tones mirror the surrounding Namib desert.

The 1975 outbreak of the Angolan Civil War brought construction to an abrupt halt and the cinema was never finished. For 50 years, it has been gradually decaying, like many other Angolan cinemas of its day. The structure has become a gathering place for the community, with people using its empty rooms for worship – and more. In 2022, news site *Ver Angola* reported that the authorities had deployed 24-hour security, after finding the building graffitied and "being used as a spa".

Despite various development proposals, including transforming it into a museum, many locals want the cinema resurrected for its original purpose. In 2025, it was added to the World Monument Fund's watchlist. The organization plans to assemble local and international stakeholders so the iconic cinema can finally realise its potential.

# Paper chase: The besieged archives of Timbuktu

**Location:**
Timbuktu, northern Mali, near the Niger River

**Threat:**
Conflict

Dating back to the thirteenth century, Timbuktu's manuscripts are an irreplaceable record of Africa's intellectual history, spanning topics from medicine to poetry. For centuries, the treasured documents have been passed on as family heirlooms. Many are held in the city's private libraries and archives, emblematic of Timbuktu's glory days as a centre of Islamic learning and trade.

In 2012, Islamist rebels took over Timbuktu and began destroying shrines. With the city's archives in danger, their priceless contents were courageously smuggled out, in an operation funded by private donors and international bodies, such as the German Foreign Office. Over an eight-month period, a small army of volunteers and librarians covertly relocated over 250,000 manuscripts to safer locations in Mali's capital, Bamako.

The ancient documents left one box at a time in canoes, carts and cars, often concealed under boxes of fruit. By the time the rebels torched two of Timbuktu's libraries in early 2013, the campaign of smuggling was well underway and only around 4,000 manuscripts were destroyed. Rebels withdrew from Timbuktu later that year and the rescue operation continued for three more months.

Since leaving Timbuktu, the papers have faced environmental threats of a different kind, including humidity, pests and inadequate storage conditions. In an attempt to preserve the manuscripts, a substantial portion has been digitised as part of a Google Arts and Culture collection called Mali Magic. With ongoing insecurity in Mali, Timbuktu's archives remain at risk. There is hope that, when there is lasting peace, the papers can return to be safely stored – and this time, they won't travel in crates of fruit.

# On the rocks: Ethiopia's eroding stone churches

At both Easter and Christmas, tens of thousands of pilgrims cloaked in flowing white arrive at the ancient churches in Lalibela, gathering in the pale dawn light to pray, chant and press their foreheads against the cold stone walls. Some have walked for weeks to reach this sacred ground, fasting along the way.

Ethiopian Orthodox Christians have worshipped at the town for 800 years. Its eleven churches were likely built by order of the twelfth-century King Lalibela, who dreamed of creating an African Jerusalem. They were not built in a traditional way, but rather were carved from solid volcanic rock, possibly to resemble the tomb of Christ. The men whose chisels carved this astonishing architecture are said to have been helped by angels.

Centuries of wind, rain, and fluctuating temperatures have begun to undo their work. Cracks snake down facades, walls crumble, and UNESCO warns that some churches are close to collapse. International heritage bodies are collaborating with the Ethiopian government to address conservation and train local priests and tradespeople in sustainable maintenance techniques. Such is the churches' spiritual significance, a stone mason must seek permission from a priest before even inserting a pin to stabilise a crumbling wall. When the pin hole is drilled, the priest collects and preserves the sacred dust.

In 2008, protective metal shelters were installed over five of the churches. The unsightly structures, nicknamed "gas station roofs" by locals, were intended to be temporary, but they still stand. Priests fear they will collapse onto the churches and plans are underway to design more harmonious alternatives. Ethiopia's Orthodox Christians believe that Christ promised the rock-hewn churches will stand strong until Judgement Day. With the dedication of priests, pilgrims and conservationists, they just might.

**Location:**
Lalibela rock-hewn churches, Amhara region, northern Ethiopia

**Threat:**
Erosion

# Reign again? Tunisia's Medieval reservoirs

**Location:**
Historic quarter of Tunis, northern Tunisia

**Threat:**
Modernization

It may lack the mystique of an ancient pyramid or the resplendence of a coral reef, but the medieval plumbing system in Tunis Medina is a treasure worth saving. It could even be a lifeline for families living there today.

Founded in 698, the Medina is the historic quarter of the Tunisian capital. Within its maze of shaded alleyways are centuries-old domed mosques, lively souks and grand doorways painted in vivid blues and greens. A UNESCO World Heritage Site, it is home to 700 or so monuments, many lavishly decorated, and around 110,000 people.

Hidden beneath the courtyards of the district's medieval homes is a long-forgotten innovation. A majel is an underground cistern that collects rain from rooftops, providing households with a means to store water. With the advent of piped water, majels fell out of use and many were destroyed, filled in, or left to crumble.

The heritage preservation organisation, World Monuments Fund (WMF), added the reservoirs of Tunis Medina to its 2025 watchlist, calling for the discarded system to be preserved and revived. Tunisia is one of the world's most water-scarce countries, with availability per capita less than a tenth of the global average. Enabling residents to store rainwater, the WMF argues, would ease pressure on the city's strained water supplies and boost the region's resilience to increasingly severe droughts.

According to the WMF, restoring the district's surviving majels will require a careful combination of traditional and modern techniques, to maintain the original infrastructure and sustainably filter rainwater. If successful, the plan would preserve part of Tunis's architectural heritage, and reinstate a lost resource for families living in the Medina, for whom every drop counts.

# Raptors in freefall: Africa's vanishing habitats

**Location:**
Raptor habitats, Sub-Saharan Africa, particularly the Sahel and Guinea forest regions of West Africa

**Threat:**
Human encroachment

In the savannas and forests of Africa, birds of prey like the red-beaked bateleur eagle were once a fairly common sight. Today, Africa's skies are growing increasingly empty of raptors, as sweeping changes reshape the landscapes below.

For millennia, raptors have inhabited diverse African ecosystems, from the semi-arid Sahel region to the verdant Congo Basin. However, rapid human population growth has dramatically altered the way this land is used. Forests have been cleared for agriculture, savannas built on, and wetlands drained for development. This seemingly relentless human expansion diminishes the natural environments that raptors depend on for hunting and nesting.

In 2024, a collaborative study co-led by the University of St Andrews found that Africa's birds of prey are facing an extinction crisis. The report shows declines among nearly 90 percent of 42 species, and warns that more than two-thirds may qualify as globally threatened. In some regions, tropical species like the martial eagle have already vanished as a direct consequence of their habitats being converted to farmland.

The decline of these birds has repercussions beyond the loss of biodiversity. Raptors help control rodent populations, and their absence can lead to an increase in these species, potentially affecting crop yields and spreading diseases. Vultures provide an unglamorous but vital ecosystem service, and their disappearance can lead to environmental contamination, as well as risks to human health. UNESCO and conservation groups are working to protect and restore critical habitats, while at the same time, promoting sustainable land-use. These efforts hold the threads of ecosystems together, for the people who depend on them.

# Fighting for breath: The Congo Basin

**Location:**
Congo Basin, spanning Central Africa, with largest portions in the Democratic Republic of the Congo and Republic of the Congo

**Threat:**
Deforestation, climate change, illegal logging and mining

Spanning six countries, the Congo Basin is one of the most important, biodiverse and vulnerable wilderness areas on the planet. Its savannas and forests teem with gorillas, elephants and various other critically endangered species, while its rainforests – nicknamed the Lungs of Africa – help mitigate climate change by absorbing colossal amounts of carbon. This delicately balanced ecosystem also provides food, shelter and medicine for millions of local and Indigenous Peoples. In fact, the Congo Basin plays a prominent role in sustaining all life on earth.

Despite their undeniable importance to the health of our planet, the Basin's forests are under threat. Unsustainable and illegal logging devastates wildlife habitats and damages local communities. Recent years have seen a resurgence of a trend for buying or leasing large areas of African land for resource extraction and export. This practice is known as land-grabbing, due to the speed and scale of the operations, and the United Nations has warned that it could jeopardise food security and lead to the loss of vital ecosystems. A growing number of agricultural developers have targeted the Basin, hoping to cash in, but new plantations – including palm oil, cocoa and rubber – often lead to even more widespread deforestation.

Both the United States and European Union have banned the illegal importing of timber, but it still flows into China, from where it is resold globally. While international organisations and government initiatives are working to preserve the forests of the Congo Basin, they face a formidable challenge. Precise predictions vary, but environmentalists agree that, without urgent action, a significant proportion of the forest could vanish within decades.

# Growing pains: Population pressure in Tanzania

**Location:**
Ngorongoro Conservation Area, northern Tanzania, near Serengeti National Park

**Threat:**
Human population growth

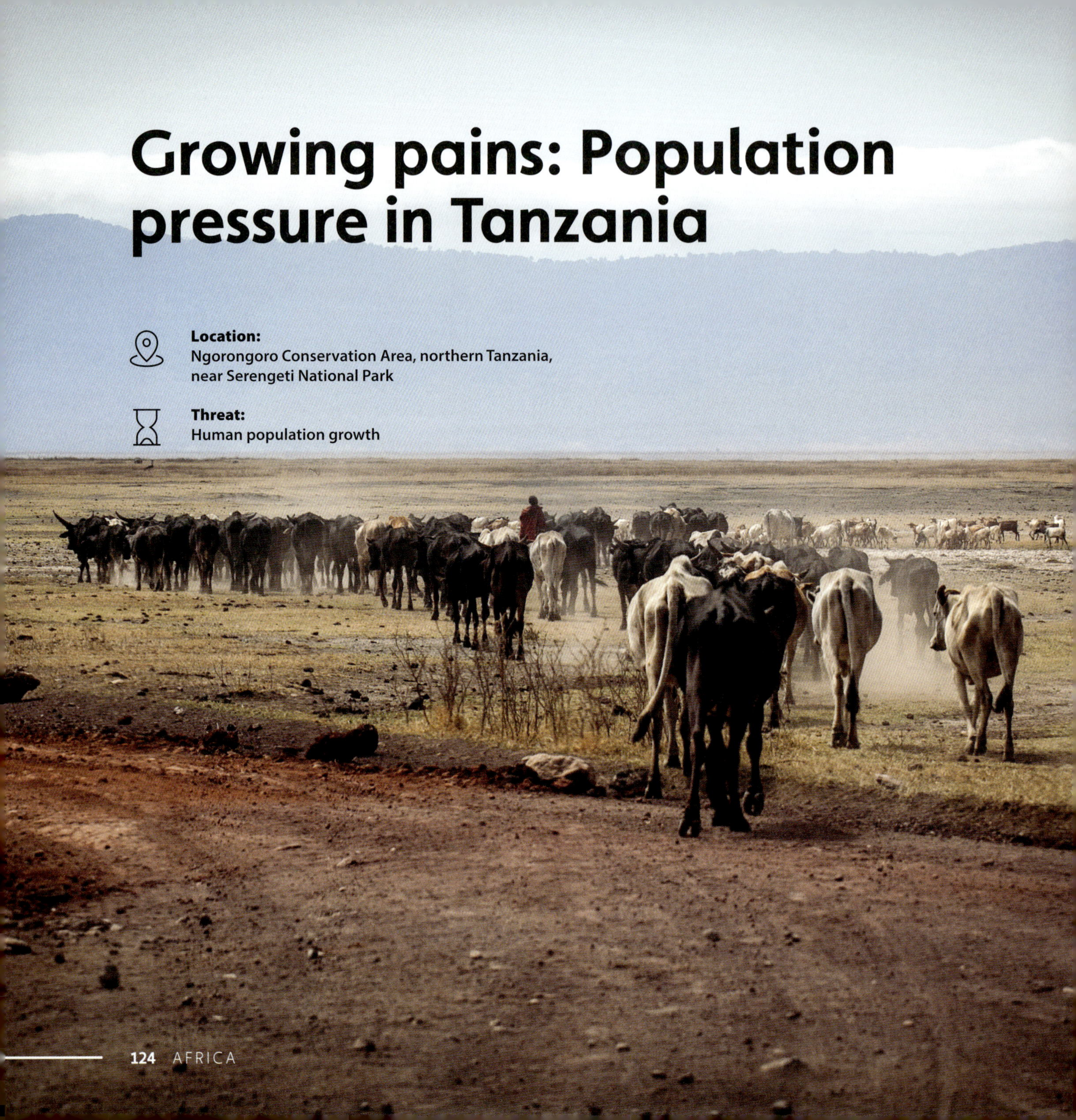

Home to leopards, lions and critically endangered black rhino, the vast volcanic crater in Tanzania's Ngorongoro Conservation Area (NCA), is one of the most important sites of large mammal biodiversity on earth. It's also a globally renowned prehistoric area, with excavations in the NCA helping to unravel the story of human evolution.

The conservation area is a UNESCO World Heritage Site that, unusually, allows people to live within its boundaries. For generations, Maasai people have lived on the land, coexisting with wildlife and practising a pastoral way of life. In recent years though, the population has grown rapidly. In 2017, 93,000 people lived in the NCA (five times as many as in 1979), and the population is predicted to grow by 73 percent by 2027, to reach 161,100.

A number of changes have fuelled the population boom, including improved health care and the growth of a tourism-driven economy. The repercussions for the NCA are far-reaching. The Maasai have long co-existed with wildlife but, as their numbers grow, land is overgrazed, disease is transferred from cattle to wildlife, and communities and cattle increasingly come into conflict with wild animals. Competition for natural resources and land has intensified and traditional Maasai building methods are giving way to modern techniques, not all of which are sustainable. More human infrastructure challenges wildlife conservation efforts and risks blocking migration routes.

If population growth continues to go unchecked, the NCA's unique harmony between humans and wildlife risks being lost. Government programmes to relocate pastoral communities outside the NCA have been met with fierce resistance. However, stricter regulations for sustainable living practices offer some hope.

# High and dry: Chad's contracting lake

**Location:**
Lake Chad, Central Africa, intersecting Chad, Nigeria, Niger and Cameroon

**Threat:**
Overuse and climate change

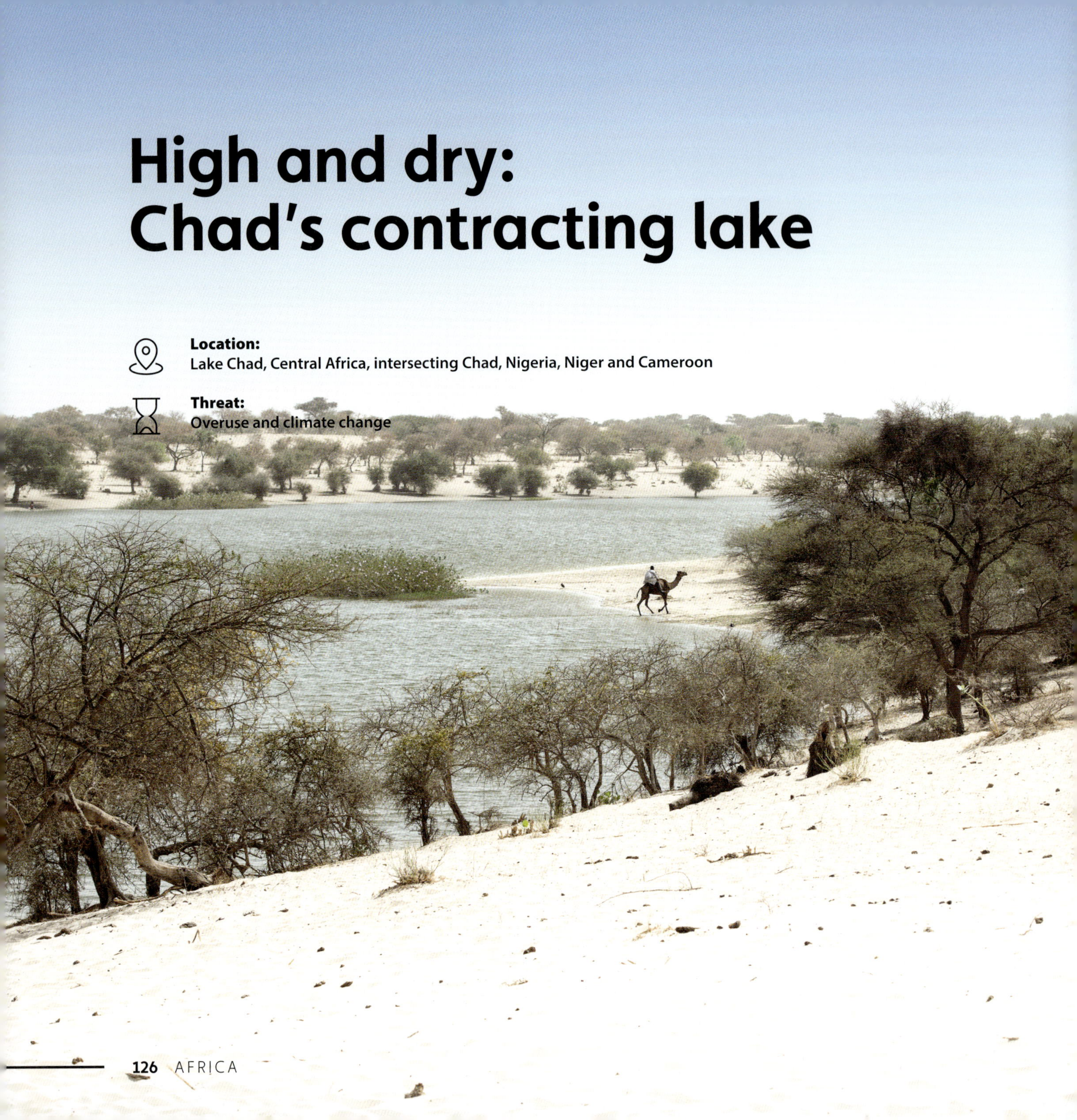

Picture a body of water the size of Israel, Puerto Rico or Belgium. Now imagine it shrinking by 90 percent over the span of three decades. Such was the fate of Lake Chad.

Bordered by Cameroon, Chad, Niger, and Nigeria, Lake Chad is a water source for millions of people in West Africa. Once the world's sixth largest lake, it began shrinking in 1963, primarily due to a reduction in rainfall, which impacted the rivers that feed the lake. Over the next three decades, a complex combination of population growth, unplanned irrigation, and climate change caused the lake to shrink further.

As Lake Chad receded, earning itself the nickname 'The Vanishing Lake', life became tougher for people living in the bordering regions. It became harder to make a living through fishing and agriculture, fuelling conflict between herders and farmers. Livelihoods, food security and health were badly affected. The gradual drying of the lake exacerbated the dire humanitarian situation in the region, and families started migrating to other areas in search of water.

Various schemes have been considered to save this vanishing lake. One proposal, known as the Transaqua Project, suggests trying to fill up Lake Chad by diverting water from the Congo River system 2,400 kilometres away – at an estimated cost of £40 billion. Sceptics point out that, in some Central African countries, governments fail to even keep the lights on consistently. The elaborate Transaqua Project, the critics warn, is a pipe dream.

While policies and plans for saving Lake Chad are thrashed out, the families living around it are in urgent need of support, as they struggle to adapt to their rapidly changing environment.

# Plant heist: South Africa's stolen succulents

When the Covid-19 pandemic shut the world indoors, an unexpected trend took root. Houseplant influencers, dubbing themselves "plant parents", flooded social media feeds with enticing greenery. Their videos sparked a global craving for exotic and resilient plants, and South Africa's Succulent Karoo biome became a prime target for a devastating illegal trade.

The Succulent Karoo is a sprawling semi-desert that stretches along South Africa's western interior and coast in muted tones of dusty gold and faded green. The arid landscape is home to over 1,500 species of small sculpture-like succulents with crimson-streaked leaves, pale jade rosettes and spirals so perfect they look hand-carved. These plants play a critical role in sustaining the biome's delicate ecosystem.

Illegal succulent harvesting has risen sharply, with criminal syndicates stripping the land and reducing millennia of growth to crumpled roots in burlap sacks. Aware that jobs are scarce, crime bosses recruit local farm workers as poorly paid poachers. The stolen succulents are posted overseas, disguised as food or toys, and sold online. South African government body, CapeNature, reported seizing more than two million poached plants between 2021 and 2024 in the Western Cape. Some species are now critically endangered.

Botanists race to restore the confiscated plants to their home. Yet, without further intervention, entire species could be wiped out. Plant-lovers can help halt demand, by using verified nurseries and reporting succulents that appear to have been harvested from the wild. South Africa's succulents have weathered centuries in the Karoo. With coordinated action by the authorities, conservationists and shoppers, they might survive the years ahead.

**Location:**
Succulent Karoo biome, Northern and Western Cape, South Africa

**Threat:**
Poaching

MERSKE

# Asia

# Overwhelmed: India's first Chinatown

**Location:**
Tiretta Bazaar neighbourhood, Kolkata, eastern India

**Threat:**
Neglect, lack of recognition

In the centre of the metropolis of Kolkata, Tiretta Bazaar is a neighbourhood with a striking story and an equally tantalizing street food scene. The Chinese immigrant community who settled in Kolkata in the eighteenth and nineteenth centuries established their homes in the area, which came to be known as Chinatown. The settlers brought their rituals, traditions and architectural styles and, over time, blended elements of Indian culture with their own. Tiretta Bazaar became a testament to Kolkata's pluralistic heritage, and is still home to a culturally distinct, but struggling, community.

There's no better way to immerse yourself in Kolkata's Chinese heritage than by sampling the delights of Tiretta Bazzar's lively food markets. Recipes, many passed through generations, blend Cantonese, other Chinese and Bengali flavours. The air is thick with the aromas of hot noodle soup, fish ball soup and juicy dumplings. Kolkata's Indo-Chinese population still gather at the neighbourhood's many Chinese temples, including the intricately carved Nam Soon temple, which dates back to the 1820s. During Chinese New Year, the streets come alive with dragon dances, beating drums and of course, feasting.

The Indo-China War of 1962 sparked the decline of Kolkata's Chinese population, a demise later exacerbated by property disputes and the marginalization of the Chinese community. Local businesses have struggled to compete with urbanization. Today, Tiretta Bazaar's ad hoc breakfast markets draw foodies from all over the city but, after breakfast, the stalls are packed up and the space becomes a car park. Developments encroach on the neighbourhood and the needs of the community are overlooked. Heritage enthusiasts fight to preserve buildings and culinary traditions. While some temples are protected, there are calls for more comprehensive preservation of this irreplaceable cultural enclave.

# The Manhattan of the Desert: Yemen's mud skyscrapers

**Location:**
Shibam, Wadi Hadramaut region, eastern Yemen

**Threat:**
Civil war, natural erosion

In Yemen's Wadi Hadramaut valley, a cluster of skyscrapers rises from the desert. Unlike most high-rises, they are built from mud and today, the sixteenth-century walled city of Shibam is one of the world's most impossible-seeming places. It's the oldest city to have been built using vertical construction, which inspired British explorer Freya Stark to dub Shibam "the Manhattan of the desert" in the 1930s.

Shibam was once an important caravan stop on the incense and spice trade routes across the southern Arabian plateau, and every inch of the historical city appears to have been meticulously designed. According to UNESCO, the city is one of the world's oldest and best examples of urban planning based on multi-storeyed construction. Surrounded by a fortified wall, Shibam's ancient high-rise buildings, some of which stand seven-storeys tall, were built using the fertile soil that surrounds the city. Unsurprisingly, these towering mud-brick marvels are extremely vulnerable. The city's buildings require ongoing upkeep and are under constant threat from erosion by rain, wind and heat, as well as from the violent civil war that erupted in Yemen in 2014.

Following a catastrophic flood in 2008, which seriously damaged a number of Shibam's buildings, a restoration programme was initiated. In the wake of the civil war, the city was also added to the UNESCO List of World Heritage in Danger. Restoration efforts are complicated by conflict and limited resources, while current political instability and security concerns make visiting the city as a tourist a challenge. Holding out against the natural and human-made dramas that threaten to engulf it, Yemen's ancient skyscraper city stands as a beacon of Islamic civilization and ingenuity.

# Last orders: Seoul's eerily empty pubs

**Location:**
Nokdu Street, Gwanak District, Seoul, South Korea

**Threat:**
Cultural shift

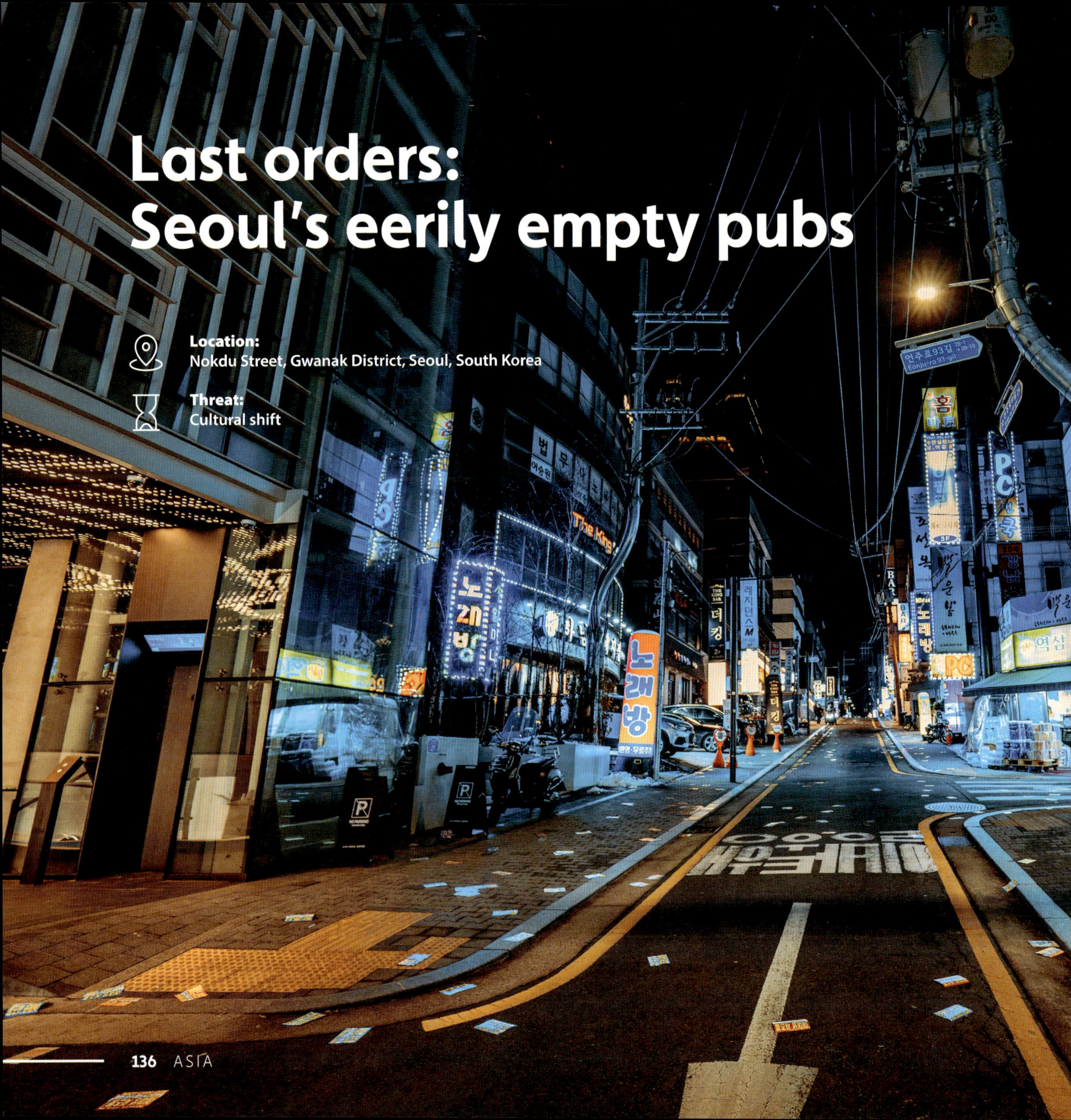

Seoul's Nokdu Street was once a favourite spot for late-night revellers. Punters spilled from packed pubs, squeezed into karaoke rooms, and played rowdy drinking games in neon-lit alleys. After long days at their desks, Seoul's office workers lined up at family-run eateries for steaming mung bean pancakes and rounds of rice wine. Today though, the same restaurants sit half-empty. Nokdu Street's karaoke booths, once overbooked, are quiet.

According to the international Organisation for Economic Co-operation and Development, alcohol consumption in South Korea has dropped by twelve percent since 2015. In some office districts, bars that once overflowed with workers are now shuttered, a sobering reminder of how the country's hard-drinking culture has shifted.

The decline has been linked to changes in South Korea's strict corporate culture, which is letting go of its tradition of *hoesik*, or after-work drinking. A 2007 High Court ruling made it an offence for senior workers to pressure subordinates into drinking, liberating youngsters from the old "drink or be fired" doctrine. Young women in particular, felt empowered to reject *hoesik*, which had, at times, encroached on their home lives and made them vulnerable to harassment. The shift towards flexible working, financial pressures caused by high interest rates, and an increasingly health-conscious mindset all contributed to workers calling time on after-work sessions.

Many of Seoul's young people say they prefer to spend their money on great food and experiences. As South Korea's policymakers grapple with the wider issue of poor domestic spending, the pubs and restaurants on Nokdu Street must adapt to their customers' changing needs. If they succeed, the iconic street can continue to be a place for fun and camaraderie – minus the hangover.

# Trouble at the top: Mount Everest

**Location:**
Mount Everest, Himalayas, Nepal-China border

**Threat:**
Climate change and overcrowding

In 2019, a viral photo exposed the world to the ugly reality of overcrowding on Mount Everest. Taken by a Nepali mountaineer, it captured a long line of climbers queuing shoulder-to-shoulder at the world's highest summit. As climbing Everest has become more accessible, the mountain has grappled with a growing human footprint. In 2023, a record number of 478 climbing permits were issued in Nepal and overcrowding reached dangerous levels. The so-called "traffic jams" that year contributed to Everest's deadliest season yet, with eighteen lives lost.

Climate change is also altering Everest's landscape. Rising temperatures on the Tibetan plateau have melted glaciers, formed lakes and replaced ice with bedrock, creating new hazards for climbers. Returning guides report rapid and unsettling transformations: ice paths have turned to water and once-solid snowfields are now dangerously soft. Even Base Camp is at risk, as melting ice threatens its stability.

Base Camp has doubled in size over recent years, due to unregulated expansion. While mountaineers of old made do with Kendal Mint Cake, today at Base Camp, clients of high-end trekking companies fortify themselves with queen-sized beds, heated tents and champagne. Critics slam the camp as a chaotic hub of commercialisation and excess, and the Nepalese authorities have pledged to enforce stricter regulations.

Other preservation strategies include limiting the number of climber permits, banning tourist helicopters, and using drones to remove the tonnes of discarded oxygen tanks and camping gear that litter the slopes. Everest has been drastically altered in the century since George Mallory gazed upon its untouched summit. Climbers continue to feel the pull of the world's highest peak, but veteran Sherpas warn Everest needs to rest.

# Shifting sands: The Maldives' dynamic islands

The Maldives is mostly known for two things – luxurious beach holidays and the likelihood that the country will one day disappear beneath the sea.

The archipelago nation is made up of 26 coral atolls and 1,192 islands, so low-lying they scarcely breach the horizon. With ice caps melting and sea levels rising, scientists have warned for decades that most of the Maldives could be underwater by the century's end. To address the vulnerability of citizens to rising tides, an artificial island called Hulhumalé was built using sand from the seabed.

However, recent scientific studies have challenged the so-called bathtub model (when water rises, everything floods). Researchers from numerous institutions, including the University of Auckland, have reported that some low-lying Maldivian islands have actually grown larger, despite the unquestionable rise in sea levels. Other islands were found to have shrunk, due to erosion caused by climate change, while most remain stable in size. This intriguing mix of shrinking, growing and stable land masses suggests the islands are dynamic.

This finding isn't to say the Maldives has nothing to fear from climate change. Indeed, the President, Mohamed Muizzu, warned as recently as 2024 that the country faces an existential threat from a climate crisis it did little to create. Rather, the islands' response to changing ocean conditions appears to be more complicated than once thought.

Scientists continue to measure currents, map waves and collect sand samples to try to understand the dynamic islands and help the government plan for coastal erosion. The country's unpredictable response to climate-related threats makes it difficult for Maldivians to prepare for the future. The islanders face the challenge of living in a place that is ever changing, for reasons beyond their control.

**Location:**
The Republic of Maldives, central Indian Ocean

**Threat:**
Climate change

# Winging it: The dying art of eagle hunting in Kyrgyzstan

**Location:**
Rural mountainous regions, eastern Kyrgyzstan

**Threat:**
Modernization

A golden eagle soars high above the windswept mountains of Kyrgyzstan. Spotting movement on the rocky hillside below, she dives with practised precision and sinks her talons into her prey. Back on her trainer's arm, the huntress is rewarded with a morsel of meat in an exchange that has bound man and bird for generations.

The nomadic people of Central Asia have used eagles to hunt for fur and food for centuries. The birds are perfectly adapted for their task, with the ability to spot prey from three kilometres away and the strength to overpower animals as large as wolves. Female chicks are taken from their nests at two or three months old – a dangerous heist that has cost men their lives when a parent eagle unexpectedly returns.

For the first few months, the hunter and bird spend most of their waking hours together. The pair then train for several years, until the eagle is ready for her first live hunt. Each bird works with only one human and their bond runs deep; so much so that archaeologists have discovered eagle bones in human burial sites. After around twenty years with their hunter, eagles are released into the wild to live out their remaining ten to twenty years.

The art of eagle hunting was nearly lost during the Soviet era, when communities were forced to abandon their nomadic lifestyle. Today, the tradition faces further threats from urbanisation and it is estimated that only a few dozen eagle hunters remain in Kyrgyzstan, a handful of whom are women. The art of falconry is recognised by UNESCO as Intangible Cultural Heritage and, in Kyrgyzstan, apprenticeship schemes have been established for young hunters. Local tourism initiatives, such as bird of prey festivals and hunting demonstrations, also play their part in preserving the ancient partnership between human and bird.

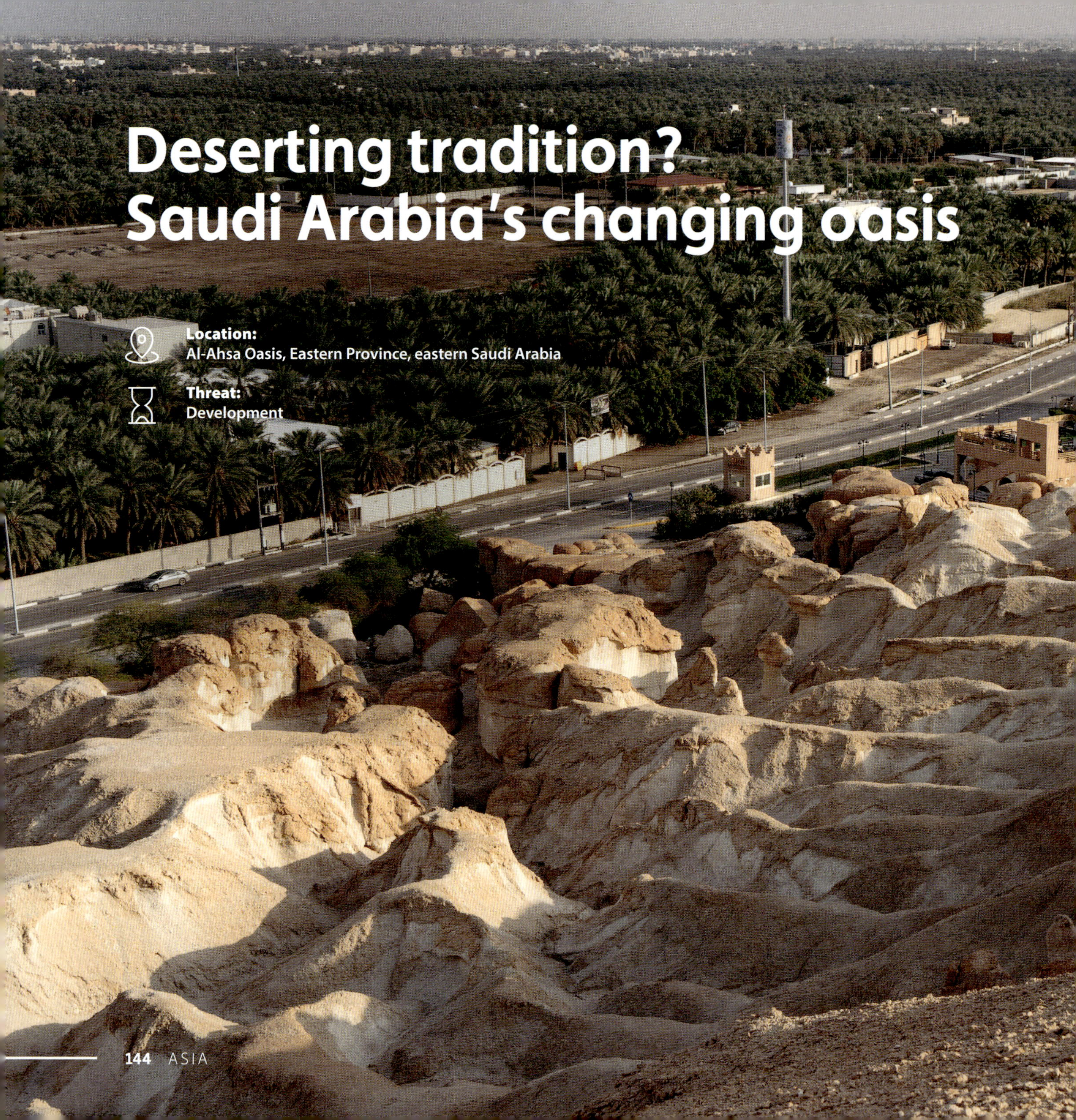

# Deserting tradition? Saudi Arabia's changing oasis

**Location:**
Al-Ahsa Oasis, Eastern Province, eastern Saudi Arabia

**Threat:**
Development

An oasis is a patch of fertile land in an otherwise arid desert. The world's largest, Al-Ahsa in Saudi Arabia's Eastern Province, is an agricultural marvel, fed by freshwater springs and farmed by local families for centuries. Its 8,500 hectares nurture an ecosystem of meandering camels, natural springs, and the two and a half million date palms that sway beneath the Arabian sun. The oasis is steeped in history, with Ottoman-era fortresses, traditional mosques, and ancient settlements dating back thousands of years. In 2018, Al-Ahsa was named a UNESCO World Heritage Site, in recognition of its ecological and historical importance.

The oasis's historic character and farming traditions are under pressure. Rapid urbanization has already consumed over 1,200 hectares of fertile terrain, as various tourism-related construction steadily encroaches. The adoption of agricultural farming techniques has dramatically changed how the land and resources are used. Mercury, arsenic and other contaminants have been detected in soil, raising questions about possible long-term risks to crops and the community. Recent studies suggest that, unless sustainable strategies are implemented, Al-Ahsa's environment could continue to deteriorate.

In November 2024, the Saudi Arabian government approved over £750 million for seventeen tourism projects in Al-Ahsa, including the creation of 1,800 hotel rooms. Plans are in place to build three resorts on a 1.8 million-square-metre plot, to be operated by United States hospitality company, Hilton. The developers say the project will establish the area as a pioneering destination for agritourism and ecotourism, while Al-Ahsa Municipality pledges to balance the demands of urban expansion with conservation. Critics can only hope the authorities and developers are true to their word.

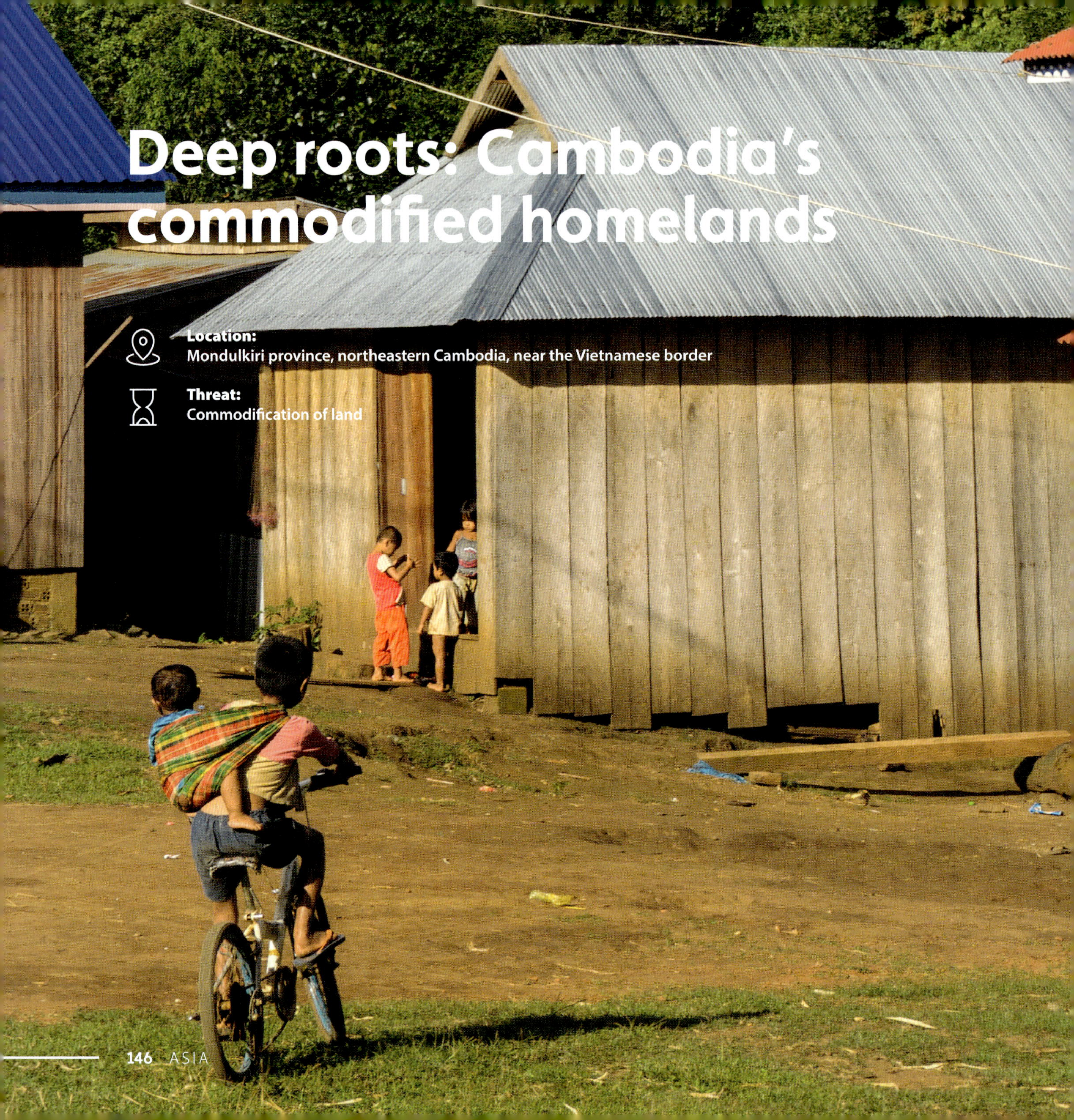

# Deep roots: Cambodia's commodified homelands

**Location:**
Mondulkiri province, northeastern Cambodia, near the Vietnamese border

**Threat:**
Commodification of land

In the rural village of Laoka, in the rugged Mondulkiri province of northeastern Cambodia, the names of local places are slowly fading from the community's memory. It's little wonder that the Bunong people here struggle to recall what they once called the land that surrounds them – after all, they no longer have access to it.

The Bunong are a marginalized Indigenous community, deeply bonded to the spirit-forests, agricultural land and traditional homes that make up their ancestral homeland. These places are woven into their identity, with profound social, spiritual, and historical significance.

For generations, the Bunong people felt free to fish, establish fields and collect forest resources where they pleased, but when bulldozers arrived in 2018, their world shifted. Their fields and forests have since been lost to the rapid expansion of rubber plantations. Sacred burial grounds, where children once learned ancestral stories, have been destroyed. The loss of land evokes painful memories of the suffering endured under the Khmer Rouge during the Cambodian Civil War (1970–75) and alcoholism and depression have surged in the community.

Yet, the Bunong people stand united, gathering to conduct ceremonies and holding meetings to mobilize against encroaching developers. Neighbours work together to cultivate what farmland remains. In 2016, the grassroots organisation Bunong Indigenous People Association (BIPA) was registered, to empower the community to protect itself from food insecurity, cultural loss and land dispossession. The struggle is far from over; longstanding legal battles with plantation owners rumble on. The Bunong people are weary, but resolute and ready to fight for the land that defines them.

# Valley of the dolls: Japan's scarecrow village

**Location:**
Nagoro village, Iya Valley, Tokushima Prefecture, western Shikoku Island, Japan

**Threat:**
Depopulation

Driving through the remote village of Nagoro, in Japan's untamed Iya Valley, you will pass scenes of flourishing village life. Men and women wait at bus stops, tend their fields and fix telephone lines. Through the schoolhouse window, children hunch over their desks. But, should you wave to any of these folk, they won't wave back.

The overwhelming majority of Nagoro's residents are made of straw. In October 2023, the village's documented population was 25 people and 350 scarecrows. Today, the number of straw figures is believed to exceed 400, each with its own name, personality and life story recorded in the scarecrow registry. Even more astonishing is that they are all made by one woman.

Tsukimi Ayano left her hometown of Nagoro, but returned after several decades in 2002 to find her once thriving village deserted. Most of her neighbours had moved to the city for work or education. Saddened by the empty streets, Ayano made a scarecrow to resemble her late father and continued making scarecrows to replace villagers as they left. In recent years, Nagoro has become a quirky tourist attraction, and Ayano now even makes celebrity scarecrows. After British TV presenter James May visited in 2019, his straw version joined the ranks.

The desertion of Nagoro reflects the broader population crisis crippling rural Japan. As countryside communities dwindle, traditional ways of life risk vanishing. Government rejuvenation programmes are trying to help villages like Nagoro but, in the meantime, individuals like Ayano are mounting their own quiet, unconventional resistance. Against all odds, Ayano has achieved her dream of repopulating her village. Thanks to her innovation and hard work, more people appear in Nagoro with every passing year – both straw and human.

# On the edge: China's viral sinkhole forests

**Location:**
Sinkholes, southern China, in limestone-rich areas of Guangxi province

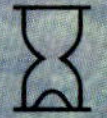

**Threat:**
Overdevelopment

Sinkholes occur when underground water dissolves limestone rock, causing the ground above to collapse. While they are generally rare, 30 have been discovered in China's Guangxi province, due to its abundant limestone. One of these great chasms, discovered in 2022, plunges nearly 200 metres into the earth. In its depths lies a hidden world of primitive forests, rare plants and animals.

Large sinkholes like this are known as *tiankeng* in Mandarin, meaning "heavenly pit". For thousands of years, they were unexplored as locals feared demons and ghosts hid within. Now, thanks to drones and a few gutsy explorers who have ventured into the gaping chasms, ecological treasures have been discovered. Sinkholes are living laboratories that preserve ecosystems for centuries, giving scientists a rare opportunity to study plants and animals they thought extinct. In Guangxi's sinkholes, researchers have found 40 metre-tall trees, previously undiscovered plant varieties, and rare species, such as ghostly white cave fish.

Videos of Guangxi's sinkholes have gone viral on social media and travellers flock to experience the thrill of abseiling into the abyss. While tourism has brought a welcome boost to the economy and infrastructure of a province only recently lifted out of poverty, scientists are concerned that revenue could be prioritised over conservation. They fear unregulated tourism could result in the loss of unique habitats and stress the need to maintain sinkholes' natural ecological states. At least one sinkhole has already been closed to protect unique orchid species.

Hot air balloons, drones and appropriately distanced pathways have been proposed, to allow tourists to observe the natural wonders in a sustainable, responsible way. However, safeguarding the long-term survival of Guangxi's extraordinary "heavenly pits" is dependent on balancing the joy of discovery with the need to protect what lies within.

# Deserted: Sharjah's Ghost Village

No one knows exactly why the residents of Al Madam abandoned their desert village, an hour's drive from Dubai, in the emirate of Sharjah.

A popular local story tells of families being forced out by supernatural spirits known as *jinns*, with some blaming Umm Al Duwais, a female *jinn* with cat-eyes and machetes for hands. A more practical explanation is that the desert's frequent and brutal sandstorms became too much for the villagers to bear.

The settlement, consisting of a dozen identical houses arranged in two rows, with a mosque at the end, was built in the 1970s. It was constructed as part of a government initiative to provide permanent housing for Bedouin tribes, during the country's push towards modernisation.

However, less than twenty years after they moved in, the residents of Al Madam all fled, leaving their village to be devoured by the desert. The empty settlement was nicknamed the Ghost Village and its decaying buildings now lie half-buried in ochre sand, shrouded in an eerie silence.

Whispers of the paranormal emerged from a rumour that the Al Madam community fled in a hurry, leaving their doors ajar and abandoning their possessions. A viral YouTube video about the legend caught the imagination of travellers and now a dozen tourists turn up each day, welcomed by tour guides who are only too happy to perpetuate ghostly rumours.

Al Madam looks set to be pulled back from the desert's grip, before it is buried entirely. In 2023, the ruler of Sharjah told local media that he plans to preserve the settlement and prepare the site for tourists. For now, curious explorers continue to enjoy unrestricted, free access to Sharjah's mysterious Ghost Village.

**Location:**
Al Madam "Ghost Village", desert near Al Madam, Sharjah, northeastern UAE, approximately 65km southeast of Dubai

**Threat:**
Desertification

# Out of fuel? Kazakhstan's aging spaceport

**Location:**
Baikonur Cosmodrome, near Baikonur, central Kazakhstan, Central Asia

**Threat:**
Geopolitics and neglect

The Baikonur Cosmodrome was once a beacon for humanity's ambition to travel beyond earth. Located in the windswept steppes of Kazakhstan, it's the world's first and largest operational facility for launching spacecraft. Built by the Soviet Union in 1955, Baikonur was originally a missile test site, but it quickly became the hub for Soviet space exploration. In 1957, it launched the first artificial satellite, *Sputnik 1*, igniting an era of discovery known as the Space Age. Four years later, Baikonur became the launch site for *Vostok 1*, which carried Yuri Gagarin on the first ever human space flight.

The spaceport became a powerful symbol of the Space Age, serving as the backbone for the Soviet, and later Russian space programmes. The Russian space agency, Roscosmos, took over managing operations from 1994, with Russia agreeing to lease the land from Kazakhstan for £93 million a year until 2050. Today, Baikonur is used for Russian launches, including manned missions to the International Space Station.

However, the cosmodrome's aging infrastructure struggles to keep pace with modern technology and maintenance costs are crippling. Political tensions between Russia and Kazakhstan have sparked disputes over property and responsibilities, while discarded rocket debris and toxic fuel are reported to have harmed local ecosystems and communities.

Yet, there is hope. The governments of Kazakhstan and Russia have collaborated on plans to assess Baikonur's environmental impact and upgrade technology. The future is uncertain, especially post-2050, but both sides want to preserve the spaceport's legacy. With investment and cooperation, there's every chance Baikonur will continue to inspire future generations to look up.

# Sliding into oblivion? Vietnam's derelict water park

**Location:**
Hồ Thủy Tiên water park, near Huế city, Thừa Thiên-Huế Province, Vietnam

**Threat:**
Neglect

The colossal dragon rising from the lake at Vietnam's abandoned Hồ Thủy Tiên water park is a sight not easily forgotten. A graffitied staircase leads up inside its hollow head to its gaping jaws, which frame a sweeping view of the park's rusted slides and crumbling aquariums.

Built in 2004, the attraction was only open for a few years. Precisely why it closed remains a mystery, though there were reports of financial difficulties and low visitor numbers. Vines and moss began reclaiming the derelict structures and the eerily beautiful park gained a cult following among urban explorers. Hồ Thủy Tiên has since featured in countless travel articles and vlogs and now thrives as an unofficial tourist attraction.

Stories and myths have flourished. Visitors report an unshakable feeling of unease while in the park. Rumours swirl that Hồ Thủy Tiên is haunted, that it's built on an ancient burial ground, and that the lake sometimes turns blood-red. Some say the park is swarming with crocodiles, which is not entirely untrue – when it closed, crocodiles released from the aquarium roamed the grounds until they were rehomed several years later.

In 2023, the land assets were sold to a private business. According to local news sources, the owner plans to dismantle attractions, including the dragon head, and hand the site over to Hue City. The Hue city government announced plans to transform Hồ Thủy Tiên into a public space, due to open in 2023, but the project has been plagued with delays. As of 2024, the derelict waterpark remains. Litter has even been cleaned up for tourists.

Time is running out to explore Hồ Thủy Tiên in its haunting, decayed condition. While the dragon looks set to vanish, taking its secrets with it, the park's future looks bright.

# Salt in the wound: The shrinking Dead Sea

**Location:**
Dead Sea, Jordan-Israel border, Middle East

**Threat:**
Water depletion

The Dead Sea flickers like a mirage in the Jordanian desert. Technically a lake, it lies 430 metres below sea level, making it the lowest place on earth. Its cobalt blue waters are ten times saltier than the ocean and inhospitable to aquatic life, giving the Dead Sea its name. The high salt content also gives the water its famous buoyancy, and thousands of tourists visit every year to float effortlessly on its surface and slather their bodies in its dark, mineral-rich mud, as Cleopatra once did.

Yet, the Dead Sea is slipping away. Hotels that once hugged the shore are now kilometres away, forced to shuttle guests to the water's edge using tractors. The water is receding by about one metre each year, and human activity is to blame. The Dead Sea's minerals are extracted for cosmetics and manufacturing, while freshwater from its main source, the Jordan River, is siphoned off for irrigation and agriculture. The retreating water causes sinkholes in the surrounding landscape, some over ten metres deep. Roads, beaches and resorts have been closed because of the risks posed by these chasms. Currently, there is no feasible way to prevent them.

An ambitious plan to save the Dead Sea by transporting water from the Red Sea via a 110-mile pipeline was deliberated for over a decade, before being abandoned in 2021. In 2024, Israel's Environmental Ministry announced a plan to restore the Dead Sea by connecting it to the Mediterranean. Another option, known as the inaction plan, is to simply allow the lake to retreat, in the expectation that it will eventually reach an equilibrium and stop shrinking. Others argue it can only be saved by prioritizing sustainable use of the Jordan River and curbing mineral extraction. While the authorities and scientists contemplate rescue plans, the ancient lake continues its retreat.

# Air of discontent: Mongolia's suffocating capital

**Location:**
Ulaanbaatar city, north-central Mongolia

**Threat:**
Air pollution

Ulaanbaatar in Mongolia is a city of extremes. The world's coldest capital, winter temperatures plummet as low as -44°C, while in summer, the city pulsates with colourful markets, a bohemian counterculture and the meditative hum of Buddhist chants.

Yet, this vibrant city is engulfed in a suffocating crisis. Ulaanbaatar is in a valley, hemmed in by mountains, so heavily polluted air becomes trapped, forcing residents to inhale it. The problem is exacerbated by the rapid population growth and deprivation in camps on the edge of the city, called ger districts.

When communism collapsed, Mongolia's rural communities lost their social support and were forced to migrate to the city for work. Over twenty per cent of the country's population is estimated to have moved to the capital, with many poor migrants living in self-built shacks and yurts in ger districts, with no plumbing or heating.

To survive Ulaanbaatar's freezing winters, families burn coal – or even tires and plastic bottles – for cooking and warmth. For decades, experts have warned that the city's dire air pollution is caused by burning coal and a lack of modern infrastructure to support clean air systems. Air samples taken in the city are over 27 times the levels deemed safe by the World Health Organization, and families pay the price with their health.

Efforts are being made on many fronts to tackle Ulaanbaatar's pollution crisis. Mongolian organizations and global development banks are financing sustainable solutions, like cleaner burning stoves, and low-cost apartments. Communities in the camps have mobilized to plant trees and make minor improvements to their living conditions. The government has pledged to halve air pollution by 2025. Frustrated by inaction, citizens hold peaceful demonstrations against the filthy air choking their city.

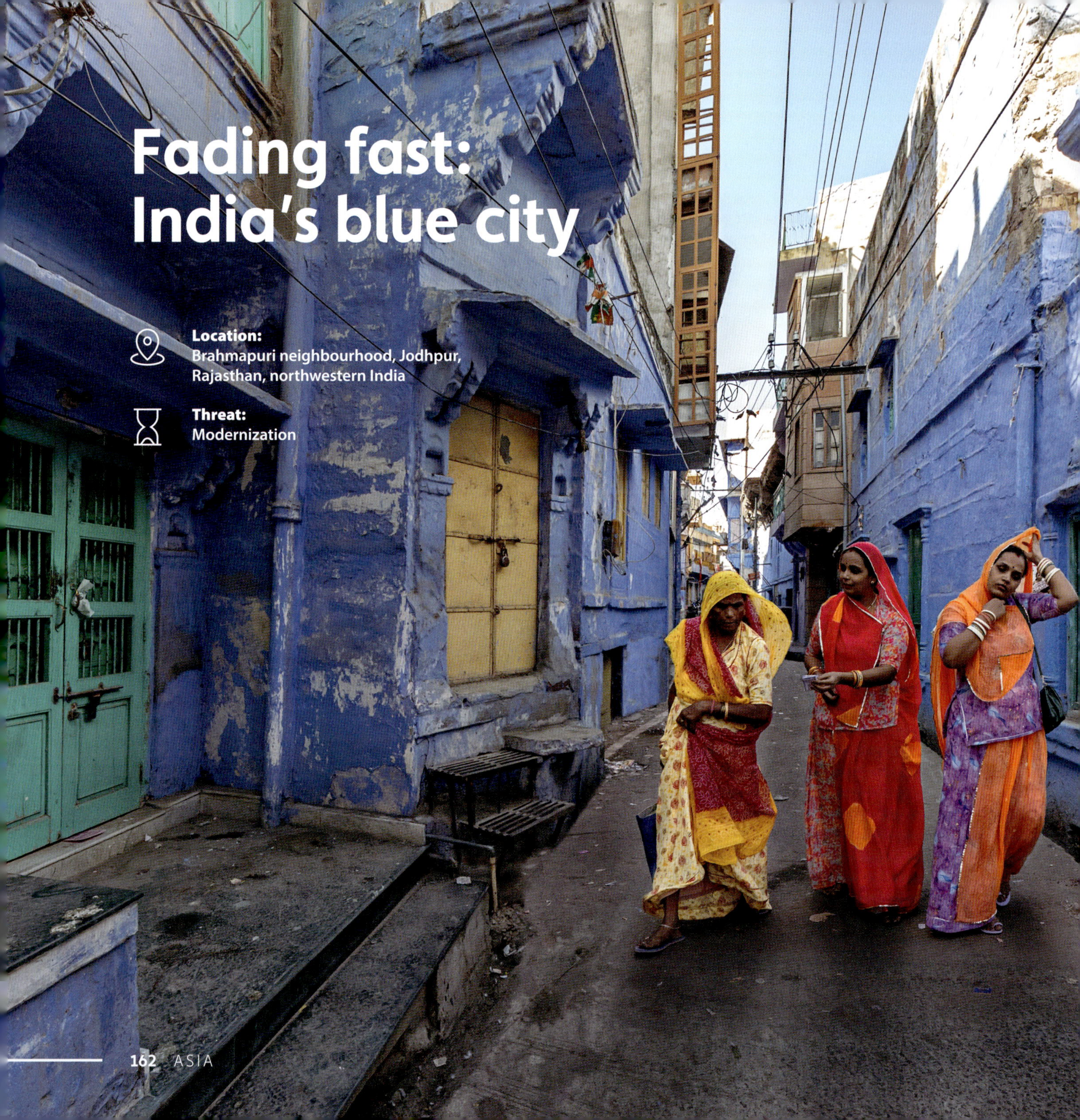

# Fading fast: India's blue city

**Location:**
Brahmapuri neighbourhood, Jodhpur, Rajasthan, northwestern India

**Threat:**
Modernization

The azure blue houses in the walled neighbourhood of Brahmapuri, in the Indian city of Jodhpur, have fascinated travellers for hundreds of years, and provided a striking background for many a selfie. Brahmapuri was built in 1459 for upper-caste families, who later adopted the colour blue for their homes as a symbol of their piety in the Hindu caste system.

As well as symbolising divinity and holy skies, the colour has other benefits. The blue pigment is a natural pest-repellent and, when mixed with limestone plaster, it cools the inside of homes. Tourist interest in Brahmapuri's indigo homes has generated a welcome source of local income.

However, unlike Morocco's famous blue city of Chefchaouen, Jodhpur's signature shade is fading, with fewer residents choosing to repaint their homes in the traditional hue. Indigo was once abundant, thanks to natural proliferation of the crop in the region, but it fell out of favour, partly due to its harmful effects on soil. The scarcity of the dye caused prices to soar. What's more, traditional lime plaster is gradually being replaced with newer building materials, such as cement or concrete, which struggle to absorb blue pigment.

In recent years, rising temperatures in Jodhpur mean that blue paint is no longer sufficient to keep houses cool. Residents, whose incomes have increased in recent years, are turning to air conditioning instead. If Jodhpur's signature colour is lost, the city's historic identity could fade, along with its appeal to tourists. Concerned community groups lobby authorities to apply lime plaster to buildings, so their walls can retain pigment. Residents fight to generate capital to save their city's heritage. So far they have raised enough funds to repaint 500 blue homes each year.

# Reduced to rubble: Beirut's battered heritage buildings

**Location:**
Gemmayzeh, Mar Mikhael, Achrafieh, and Saifi neighbourhoods, Beirut, Lebanon

**Threat:**
Neglect

On 4th August 2020, one the largest non-nuclear explosions in history tore through Beirut. Houses crumbled and glass rained from the sky. At least 218 residents were killed and over 300,000 lives were uprooted.

The blast, caused by improperly stored ammonium nitrate, ripped through the soul of the city. It destroyed or damaged over 600 historic buildings, mainly in the neighbourhoods of Gemmayzeh, Mar Mikhael, Karantina and Ashrafieh. These areas of rich architectural heritage were home to the Ottoman-era mansions of Beirut's 19th-century elite, as well as elegant French and modernist designs of the early twentieth century. Their iconic facades, featuring graceful arches framed by marble columns, once opened to grand central halls filled with life. Many of these buildings were reduced to rubble. Those that remain are badly damaged and risk being demolished for redevelopment, irreversibly altering the historic character of Beirut.

The United Nations agency, UN-Habitat, has launched a project to restore four damaged heritage residences, including nineteenth-century mansion Villa Mokbel, which is rumoured to be reopening as a boutique hotel. UNESCO and the Beirut Heritage Initiative have provided restoration guidance, including manuals tailored to Ottoman-period buildings. However, Beirut's heritage buildings face major ongoing challenges. Lebanon's economic crisis and the ongoing fall-out from the 2024 Israel-Hezbollah conflict continue to stall preservation projects. Many important buildings remain at risk.

Restoring the city to its former glory requires large-scale protective policies, planning strategies, and substantial funding. Beirut has a long history of overcoming adversity. The city has rebuilt before; there is hope it will rise again.

# Royally ruined: Emperor Jahangir's tomb

When a 400-year-old mausoleum has had to contend with centuries of pillaging, flooding and encroachment by its urban neighbours, it's a wonder it's still standing. The ancient tomb of Emperor Jahangir, on the banks of the Ravi River near Lahore, is a celebrated marvel of Mughal architecture. It was finally completed in 1637, after a gruelling decade-long construction. Despite being among the world's most powerful men, Emperor Jahangir is said to have preferred immersing himself in nature to waging wars. His tomb was built according to his wish, in his beloved pleasure garden, Dilkusha.

The facade of red sandstone and meticulously-laid white marble is a vision of dignified simplicity, giving no hint of the riot of colour that awaits within. Inside, dazzlingly intricate tiled mosaics and vibrant frescoes adorn every corner of the walls, floor and ceiling. The tomb's splendour attracted the attention of Ranjit Singh, during Sikh rule. In the early nineteenth century, it was pillaged by his army and later used as a private residence for Sikh army officer, Señor Oms. The tomb and surrounding complex were further damaged when the Lahore-Peshawar Railway Line was built under British rule.

While the tomb is not yet a UNESCO World Heritage Site, the Federal Antiquities Act of 1975 forbids construction within 60 metres. However, as Shahdara city has grown more densely populated, these stipulations have been ignored. Today, private homes sit shoulder-to-shoulder a few metres from the monument's boundary wall. What's more, the site's foundations have been weakened by periodic floods. The southeast section was washed away, likely in the nineteenth century. Later, in 1988, another major flood submerged the area in 3.5 metres of water for five days. Sporadic restoration efforts have been carried out over the years, but for Jahangir's remarkable tomb to endure, there is more work to do.

**Location:**
The Tomb of Jahangir, Shahdara Bagh precinct, near Lahore, Punjab, northeastern Pakistan

**Threat:**
Neglect

# A world within: China's only cave village

**Location:**
Zhongdong Village, Zhong Cave, Guizhou Province, southern China

**Threat:**
Forced relocation

To reach their nearest town, families living in Zhongdong village must walk for two and half hours along winding mountain paths. Their home lies inside a remote cave, hidden in the hills of southwest China. Fewer than twenty families, descendants of the Miao ethnic minority, share a space the size of a football stadium.

The Miao people moved into the cave during the Chinese Civil War to evade bandits. When conflict ended, they chose to stay, embracing a life of rustic isolation. Simple houses are built from wood and woven bamboo near the cave entrance. They don't need roofs, as the cave protects them from the elements. It provides natural insulation too, staying warm in winter and cool in summer. Rainwater drips continuously from gaps in the rock, acting as a natural water source.

For nearly seven decades, the cave community has lived off the land, raising livestock and growing corn in the fields outside, which they sell at the nearest market, fifteen kilometres away. In 2003, an American hiker discovered the cave and donated funds for electricity. Now, a few washing machines, lights and TVs embellish the otherwise simple lives of the residents.

In a bid to fulfil its promise to eliminate poverty, the Chinese government has cleared many poor mountain villages, offering farmers new homes in towns. Zhongdong risks being next. A few years ago, the villagers came close to handing the cave over to the government to turn into a tourist attraction. However, when the government-built houses at the foot of the mountain did not match what the villagers had been promised, they refused to leave. For now, Zhongdong residents continue their cave-dwelling lifestyle, but officials say it's not inconceivable that the villagers may one day be forcibly removed.

# Brace for turbulence: Japan's sinking airport

**Location:**
Kansai International Airport, artificial island, Osaka Bay, southwestern Japan

**Threat:**
Subsidence

The first airport to be built entirely on an artificial island, Japan's Kansai International Airport is a landmark of civil engineering. The bold – and untested – plan of building an airport offshore was hatched when Japan's second-largest city, Osaka, outgrew its airport with no room to expand on land. Kansai was subsequently built on reclaimed land in Osaka Bay, connected to the mainland by a bridge. It remains one of the most ambitious engineering projects of its kind.

In the three decades since it opened, the airport has survived several natural disasters, including the Great Hanshin earthquake of 1995 and Typhoon Jebi in 2018. In a testament to its design and construction, the building emerged from both relatively unscathed. Kansai's terminal building was once the world's longest and the airport boasts a practically perfect record of luggage management. Yet, despite its many achievements, Kansai faces a significant hurdle – the land under it is sinking. At the time of construction, engineers anticipated the ground would subside, but it is happening much faster than predicted. The problem is linked to the land's unpredictable deep clay layer, which has been compared to a wet sponge.

Over £100 million has been spent on efforts to keep the island above sea level, including raising the sea wall. However, without more significant intervention, parts of the artificial island are expected to sink to sea level by 2056. Some experts warn it's already too late to save the airport, predicting that the financial burden of keeping it operational will eventually outweigh the benefits.

Kansai's radical design paved the way for other offshore airports and it remains one of Asia's busiest terminals. Although a question mark looms over its future, Kansai's legacy as a marvel of engineering remains on sure footing.

# Shattered: Afghanistan's Bamiyan Valley

Afghanistan's high-altitude Bamiyan Valley has a long and influential history, the past few decades of which have been marred by tragedy. The region has been settled for thousands of years and, by the mid-sixth century, around 2,000 monks lived and worshipped in Buddhist monasteries in the foothills of the valley. Around that time, several colossal statues of the Buddha – including the world's tallest at 55 metres – were carved into the towering sandstone cliffs. The caves nearby were adorned with murals, among the world's oldest known oil paintings.

Decades of conflict have rendered this remarkable place unsafe. In 2001, the world watched helplessly as – over several days – the Taliban used a range of tanks, dynamite and rockets to destroy the ancient statues, which they decreed to be forbidden idolisations of Buddha. Local workers were forced to embed the explosives and international journalists fought to contain their emotion as they reported on the worst act of cultural terrorism in their lifetimes.

While the obliteration of the Buddhas was vehemently denounced by the international community, ongoing conflict in the region prevented major attempts to rebuild them. Over time, the Buddhas' outlines and few remaining features have been degraded by neglect, unauthorised excavations, and their reported use in target practice by Taliban gunmen.

Since regaining control of Afghanistan in 2021, the cash-strapped Taliban has attempted to promote the Bamiyan Valley as a tourist destination, but international governments warn against travel. Bamiyan is a UNESCO World Heritage In Danger Site, and numerous local and global agencies have initiated ambitious projects to protect it. However, resources are often lacking and with threats from neglect, looting and civil unrest, what remains of the ancient site is extremely fragile.

**Location:**
Bamiyan Valley, Hindu Kush mountains, central Afghanistan, approximately 230km northwest of Kabul

**Threat:**
Neglect

# Oceania

# Lost? Stick chart navigation in the Marshall Islands

**Location:**
Marshall Islands, central Pacific Ocean, between Hawaii and Australia

**Threat:**
Modernization

Stick charts have a misleading name. They are not made from sticks, nor were they used as maps as we understand them today. Long before GPS or modern mapping techniques, the seafarers of the Marshall Islands in the central Pacific Ocean relied on stick charts to navigate the islets and atolls of their island nation. These intricate frameworks, made from the stems of coconut leaves and shells, mapped the unseen rhythms of the sea, encapsulating the wisdom of Marshallese navigators.

Used from ancient times until the early twentieth century, stick charts are notoriously difficult to decipher. Anthropologists have arrived at a general understanding of the abstract ways they represent currents, wind and wave patterns and the locations of atolls and islands. However, many stick charts can only be fully interpreted by their creators. A type known as *mattang* illustrated general ocean characteristics and was used to train the younger generation of seafarers. Another style, *meddo*, provided navigational instructions, although they were not to scale so distances were not accurate. Both were very fragile and neither was taken on journeys. Instead, they were memorized.

The advent of modern navigation technologies, coupled with a decline in traditional canoe voyages, has led to the loss of much traditional navigation knowledge in Micronesian culture. With fewer seafarers learning how to create and read stick charts, this unique skillset risks disappearing. While their practical use fell away long ago, stick charts remain culturally important to Marshallese people and efforts are underway to preserve the technique. Scientists, communities and heritage organisations, such as the Alele Museum and Public Library in Majuro, are attempting to document and teach stick chart practices. If conservation efforts and local enthusiasm prevail, this ancient navigation art won't end up uncharted.

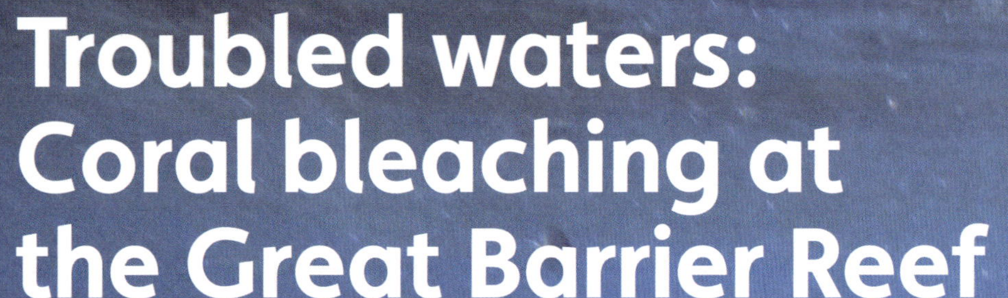

# Troubled waters: Coral bleaching at the Great Barrier Reef

**Location:**
Great Barrier Reef, Queensland coastline, northeastern Australia, stretching over 2,300 kilometres in the Coral Sea

**Threat:**
Climate change

Australia's Great Barrier Reef is a global icon. A mesmerizing mosaic of colour larger than Italy, it's the world's biggest coral reef. It supports thousands of species of marine life and over 60,000 jobs, yet it faces an existential threat.

One of the greatest threats to the reef's survival is coral bleaching, caused when rising ocean temperatures weaken and potentially kill coral. In 2024, the reef suffered one of the worst bleaching events on record, sending shockwaves worldwide. University of Sydney scientists found more than 40 percent of corals near One Tree Island in the southern reef were killed that year. Coral bleaching, their report warns, has reached catastrophic levels. Without action, some models predict the reef's ecosystem will vanish within 30 years.

Just two years earlier, hope was sparked when sections of the reef showed record levels of coral cover. However, the full picture is more complicated. While the reef appeared to be healing, much of the new growth was Acropora coral – a fast-growing genus, but easily destroyed by storms and predatory starfish. What's more, within a year the recovery had stalled, according to the Australian Institute of Marine Science.

Science and technology innovations offer hope. An engineering expert from the University of Cambridge – inspired, he says, by *Finding Nemo* – is working with Australian researchers to explore a technique called marine cloud brightening. This involves spraying fine seawater droplets into the atmosphere so clouds reflect more sunlight, thereby cooling the ocean surface and mitigating bleaching. Meanwhile, an Australian non-profit environmental organisation, the Great Barrier Reef Foundation, is trying to future-proof the reef by growing heat-resilient corals. The loss of this iconic reef would be felt far beyond the Queensland coast. Saving it, through innovation, conservation and climate action, requires a global effort.

# Rocky outlook: Easter Island's vulnerable icons

**Location:**
Easter Island (Rapa Nui), a territory of Chile, southeastern Pacific Ocean

**Threat:**
Climate change

Easter Island, or Rapa Nui, is a world-famous speck in the Pacific Ocean. The small island is home to nearly 900 monolithic statues, known as moai, carved from volcanic rock. Shrouded in mystery, these figures are believed to have been created by the Indigenous Rapa Nui people between the thirteenth and sixteenth centuries. No figures quite like them have been found anywhere else.

Ranging from four to ten metres tall, the moai have disproportionately large heads with elongated faces, heavy brows and solemn expressions. They were believed to have been figures of spiritual devotion for the Rapa Nui, each the incarnation of a prominent ancestor. Positioned predominantly along the coastline, the moai face inland, eternally watching over the descendants of those they depict.

In October 2022, a devastating forest fire, intensified by prolonged drought conditions linked to climate change, caused significant damage to several moai, prompting global concern for their preservation. Rising sea levels and increased coastal erosion weaken the statues' foundations, threatening to destabilize them. The Indigenous Rapa Nui community, alongside international organizations, has initiated preservation efforts. Biochemical treatments have been applied to strengthen the stone, and a sea wall has been built to preserve the moai on the island's southern coast.

Additionally, researchers are exploring building drainage systems, to help mitigate water damage during heavy rains, and using climate-resilient vegetation to stabilize the soil around the statues. All these projects depend partly on tourism revenue, which suffered a huge setback during the pandemic. Now, the eyes of the world are on the tiny island of Rapa Nui, hoping its mysterious moai can survive, to continue their vigil.

# Uprooted: Indonesia's last treetop homes

**Location:**
Korowai treehouse villages, Papua rainforests, Indonesia, on the island of New Guinea

**Threat:**
Modernization

For generations, the Indigenous Korowai people have built towering treehouses in the rainforests of Papua, on the isolated island of New Guinea. Until the 1970s, the Korowai had little or no contact with other people.

The community has a deep connection to the forest, relying on it for hunting, fishing and horticulture. Their treetop homes, some up to 40 metres high, are constructed using basic tools and expert climbing skills. Living high above the ground protects the Korowai from disease-carrying mosquitoes, floods and, they believe, evil spirits.

The Korowai have long been a source of fascination for outsiders, but myth and sensationalism have often obscured reality, and some documentary-makers have misrepresented them. A 2011 episode of the BBC's *Human Planet* featured treehouses that were later revealed to have been fabricated for filming, raising troubling questions about the impact of outside influences and the ethics of attempting to document a so-called untouched tribe. Prior to the BBC film, media coverage tended to sensationalize the controversial myth that Korowai people still practice cannibalism. In fact, anthropologists suspect the tradition has ended among Korowai groups who have regular outside contact.

In the last 40 years, the Korowai have been introduced to new religions, tourism and modern influences, and faced threats from deforestation and disease. Some moved to villages built by the government or missionaries. Fewer than 4,000 Korowai people are estimated to remain in the rainforest, dubbed the last generation. Time will tell whether this unique treetop life is really on the cusp of vanishing, or whether that's another myth.

# The stuff of legend: Micronesia's secret city

In a lagoon close to Pohnpei Island, in the Pacific Ocean, mangrove forests hide a secret that has beguiled historians and archaeologists for centuries.

Beneath the tangled canopy is the ancient city of Nan Madol. The sprawling complex of nearly 100 man-made islets, linked by canals, was built around the year 1200. Its structures are made from colossal basalt pillars, some weighing as much as an elephant. Astonishingly, the rocks are not native to the area. Even with today's technology, transporting them would be a challenge. How an ancient civilization accomplished it remains one of history's most tantalizing mysteries.

Legends swirl about Nan Madol's construction. Some say giants built it, others speak of dragons. A popular local tale tells how twin brothers, Olisihpa and Olosohpa, used sorcery to move the stones. Nan Madol remains shrouded in secrecy. Before visiting, travellers have even reported seeking permission from the King of Pohnpei and partaking in a ceremonial *kava* drink, made from roots ground on an ancient pounding stone.

Nan Madol is recognised by UNESCO, both for its historical value and its vulnerability. Structures are being damaged by encroaching vegetation and their foundations are weakened by tropical storms. Natural erosion threatens to destroy what remains of the city. In recent years, researchers have used advanced scanning technology to penetrate the undergrowth and build a fuller picture of what lies beneath. Such scans have revealed 90 previously hidden structures, along with an 800-year-old pounding stone similar to those used to make *kava* today.

As international conservation teams race to discover and protect the ancient site, it remains a powerful symbol of the allure of the unknown. For now, the future of Nan Madol is as much a mystery as its past.

**Location:**
Nan Madol, eastern coast of Pohnpei Island, Federated States of Micronesia

**Threat:**
Erosion

# Living landmarks: Australia's culturally modified trees

**Location:**
Modified trees, First Nations territories, including Gamilaraay country, New South Wales, Australia

**Threat:**
Land clearance

On an arid, open plain in northern New South Wales (NSW), an old leopardwood tree grows in the sandy soil. Its branches, spotted like a leopard's coat, have been manipulated to form a ring, serving as a message to travellers that a reliable water source is nearby.

This is Gamilaraay country, the traditional lands of the Gamilaraay people, one of Australia's largest Aboriginal language groups. The leopardwood is one of many trees to have been manipulated by Aboriginal people to share knowledge. Young branches were bound, twisted and shaped while growing, to turn trees into rings or arrows. Trunks were carved into bowls to hold water for parched travellers and branches were plaited to signify kinship.

Modern researchers have dubbed these trees culturally modified trees (CMTs). To First Nations people, their meaning runs deep. Each tree has an identity, a role in the community and a spirit. However, all over Australia, trees shaped by the hands of Aboriginal people are vanishing due to agricultural expansion.

In NSW, some CMTs are protected under the National Parks and Wildlife Act 1974, but others have no legal protection. One unprotected variety grows in the bright red soil of Wailwan country, in northern NSW, and is known as a tree-in-a-tree. Aboriginal people planted a tree when a person was born and then a second, within the trunk of the first, when that person died. Locals campaign for legislative recognition of trees-in-trees and have recorded around 1,000 examples in northern NSW and Queensland.

While no tree can last forever, campaigners fight for those altered by Aboriginal peoples to be protected as living cultural heritage, so their stories and spirits can endure for as long as possible.

# Shell-shocked: The Solomon Islands' dead lagoon

**Location:**
Langa Langa Lagoon, west coast of Malaita Island, Solomon Islands

**Threat:**
Unsustainable fishing practises

A cultural symbol of the Solomon Islands, shell money is made by smoothing broken shells into discs and stringing them together. The value of a string of shells is based on the time and skill required to create it. Although the Solomon Islands dollar became their official currency in 1977, islanders still use shell money to settle disputes and buy land. What's more, there is a community that still depends on the production of shell money for its income. Known as saltwater people, shell money producers live on small artificial islands built on sandbars in the Langa Langa Lagoon. Their lives and livelihoods are intrinsically tied to the lagoon's marine ecosystem, which faces a grave threat.

Dynamite fishing has obliterated coral reefs and mangroves, essential habitats for fish and shells. The destructive practice has caused a critical loss of biodiversity in the lagoon and an 80 percent decline in seashell numbers. Divers report that the once vibrant coral reefs are drained of colour, earning Langa Langa the nickname "the dead lagoon". Shell money-makers are forced to buy shells from other provinces, for up to £50 a bag. Unable to sustain their craft, some have turned to dynamite fishing (the very thing that put them out of business), perpetuating the cycle of environmental destruction. Unexploded World War II bombs scattered across the Solomon Islands provide a ready source of dynamite, but the dangerous process of extracting and using the explosives has cost fishermen their limbs.

Painfully aware of the damage wrought by dynamite fishing, locals are calling for government-funded schemes to help them transition to other industries. For now though, the Langa Langa Lagoon community is caught in a vicious cycle, trying to find a sustainable income that doesn't jeopardize their cultural heritage and the ecosystem that they and their children depend on.

# The Pacific's underwater timebomb: Chuuk Lagoon

**Location:**
Chuuk Lagoon, Federated States of Micronesia, western Pacific Ocean

**Threat:**
Structural decay

One morning in 2022, families living on Guadalcanal island in the Solomon Islands woke to find the sea and shore smothered in an inky black mass. Paddling out in canoes to investigate, they discovered oil bubbling up from the ocean floor. It almost certainly leaked from one of the many sunken shipwrecks along the island's coastline.

World War II left a legacy of over 3,800 shipwrecks abandoned on the floor of the Pacific Ocean. The bulk of them are in Chuuk Lagoon, an idyllic barrier reef lagoon in the Federated States of Micronesia. Once a wartime Japanese base, the area is now the world's largest ship graveyard. Although the wrecks have provided locals with an income from tourism, they threaten to endanger their lives and livelihoods. The sunken ships still hold a toxic cargo of thousands of tons of oil and possibly unexploded munitions. Sitting underwater for more than 80 years, their hulls are thinning and scientists warn that nineteen vessels are at risk of imminent collapse.

Many of the wrecks flagged as pollution risks are already leaking oil. Divers report seeing little black bubbles seeping from the rusting hulls and eaten by fish. In the event of a major spill, oil is guaranteed to smother both sea and land. The lagoon's communities depend almost entirely on the ocean. Past spills, such as 2010's Deepwater Horizon catastrophe, leave them in no doubt about the devastating impact of such a disaster.

Safeguarding the lagoon will require collaboration by multiple governments. In August 2024, the United States and Japanese authorities announced they will explore a joint effort to remove oil from the sunken ships. However, some wrecks are predicted to collapse as soon as 2026, so for the people and marine life of Chuuk Lagoon, the clock is ticking.

BOYS. HOME

# Space to heal: Kinchela's boys' home

Some are now well into their 80s or 90s, yet the survivors of the notorious Kinchela Aboriginal Boys Training Home cannot forget what they endured there as children. Between 1924 and 1970, an estimated 600 Aboriginal boys aged five to fifteen were kidnapped from their families and incarcerated at the Government-run facility. The boys were subjected to barbaric and dehumanizing programmes intended to strip them of their culture and assimilate them into white society.

Upon arrival, each boy's name was replaced with a number. Forced to undertake hours of gruelling farm labour, the boys' daily lives were characterized by physical hardship, alienation, abuse and punishment. Survivors recall being chained to a fig tree for days at a time, as a brutal form of discipline. The tree and chain are still there, but the tree has slowly grown to smother the metal, leaving just two rusted links still visible, embedded in its trunk.

The facility was finally closed in 1970 and the children incarcerated there and at similar institutions came to be collectively known as Australia's Stolen Generations. Survivors, their families and communities have had to endure painful multi-generational trauma. Many now see the home's vacant and decaying site as an important place of truth-telling and healing. A survivor-run group, the Kinchela Boys Home Aboriginal Corporation, is working with architects on a plan to transform it into a support centre and museum to address the legacy of violence against the Stolen Generations.

The survivors group hoped the museum would open in time to mark the centenary of the facility's opening, in 2024, but construction has not yet started. As survivor numbers diminish, time is running out to record their stories and prevent the truth about the Stolen Generations fading from Australian history.

**Location:**
Kinchela Aboriginal Boys Training Home, near Kempsey, New South Wales, Australia

**Threat:**
Abandonment

# Tuvalu: the world's first Digital Nation?

**Location:**
Tuvalu, central Pacific Ocean, midway between Hawaii and Australia

**Threat:**
Climate change

In 2021, a government minister from Tuvalu, Simon Kofe, addressed the UN Climate Change Conference (COP26) via video from the nation's capital, Funafuti. Wearing a suit and tie, Kofe stood knee-deep in seawater. "We are sinking", he told the world.

Of all the small island nations at risk from climate change, Tuvalu's situation is among the most urgent. The small Pacific Ocean nation, made up of nine coral islands, is one of the world's lowest-lying countries. With current sea level rises, some estimates predict that half the land in the capital will be underwater in three decades, comfortably within the lifetimes of young islanders.

As the sea carves up Tuvalu's shores, its people face an existential choice: What to do? Try to defend their homes from flooding? Build new land? Evacuate? These have all been considered, but Tuvalu's government has another strategy for preserving land, culture and sovereignty.

A year after Kofe's powerful COP26 address, Tuvalu's government announced that it is building a digital clone of the nation. The Digital Nation project aims to back up everything, from homes to trees, using drones and 360-degree cameras. Efforts to map every inch of the island began in 2023. A recording team drove mopeds down narrow streets and, when the paths became too tight, they walked with handheld GoPros. The project intends to record the island's soul too, with citizens asked to submit their favourite memories, dances and songs, and the stories told to them by grandparents.

The final goal is to preserve sovereignty. The project seeks to create digital passports, which would preserve government functions and national identity in the event that Tuvalu's land disappeared. No one knows precisely what fate awaits Tuvalu's landmass but, thanks to Digital Nation, islanders at least have access to their memories, and possibly legal protection too.

# Turning the tide: Teahupo'o's endangered reef

**Location:**
Teahupo'o, southwestern coast of Tahiti, French Polynesia, South Pacific Ocean

**Threat:**
Development and over-fishing

Just off the shore, near the remote village of Teahupo'o on Tahiti's southwestern coast, is a turquoise lagoon. The water is encircled by a kaleidoscopic coral reef that teems with marine life and holds huge ecological value. For locals, the reef provides a larder, an income and a playground. Generations have fished and performed rituals there, building lives deeply entwined with the ocean.

Beyond the lagoon's edge is one of the world's best reef breaks, where waves crash dramatically over the coral. During the Paris 2024 Olympic Games, surfers from around the world gathered in Teahupo'o to go for gold. The competition was the culmination of a year of intense construction in the village, which locals feared would irreversibly harm the reef. The delicate ecosystem had already been weakened by overfishing and unsustainable tourism.

The infrastructure proposals prompted outcry from the community. Locals pushed back, particularly on the plan to build an aluminium judging tower in the lagoon. Their protests were heard and a more environmentally-friendly tower was built instead. Nevertheless, the new tower design still disturbed the coral. Time will tell the extent of the damage, but, had it not been for fierce local resistance, the reef would have suffered far more.

The people of Teahupo'o have rallied in other ways to protect the reef, which has been hit hard by years of over-fishing. Community leaders have reintroduced the traditional prohibition practice of *rahui*, a temporary ban on fishing to allow the reef to heal. Coral Gardeners, an environmental organisation made up of surfers, freedivers and fishermen, partners with locals to regrow damaged corals and educate youngsters on sustainable stewardship. For the people of Teahupo'o, the underwater world is a lifeline that they will fight to defend.

# Swamped: New Zealand's wounded wetlands

**Location:**
Whangamarino Wetland, Lower Waikato Basin, North Island, New Zealand

**Threat:**
Wildfires and human activity

In the waterlogged soil of the Waikato wetlands, a bird the size of a buzzard stands upright and motionless, its feet sinking into the spongy ground and its beak pointing skyward. The Australasian bittern is just one of the endangered species that breed in this expansive mosaic of swamps, bogs and shallow lakes on New Zealand's North Island. These wetlands are also home to the critically endangered swamp helmet orchid, whose tiny hood-shaped flowers are not found anywhere else on earth.

Whangamarino is the second largest wetland on the North Island and one of New Zealand's biggest carbon sinks, meaning it absorbs more carbon dioxide from the atmosphere than it releases. It is therefore crucial to mitigating global warming. Wetlands like this were once common throughout New Zealand's lower Waikato Basin and Hauraki Plains regions. Today, fewer than twenty percent of original freshwater wetlands remain, and they are one of the country's most threatened ecosystems.

The Whangamarino wetland has been dramatically altered by urban development, agriculture and pollution, while the introduction of non-native species has harmed the health of the ecosystem. A 2024 fire scorched around 1,000 hectares, devastating wildlife and releasing stored carbon into the environment. According to the Department of Conservation, environmental recovery could take decades.

The wetland is protected through the Waipā Peat Lakes and Wetlands Accord, an agreement signed by local councils, *iwi* (Māori kinship groups), conservationists and other agencies. Despite ongoing environmental pressures, the committee is working to restore habitats and promote sustainability, so that species like the Australasian bittern can continue to thrive.

# Rock bottom: Australia's forgotten gold mines

**Location:**
Llanelly and Tarnagulla towns, Victoria Goldfields, central Victoria, Australia

**Threat:**
Loss of industry

The abandoned Welsh mining village of Llanelly is located, somewhat unexpectedly, in southeastern Australia. Sensational gold discoveries in the region in the 1860s lured young miners from Wales, who were rewarded with an abundance of gold. They established a village, named after their hometown, with schools, banks, hotels and shops to serve the Welsh-speaking community. In its glory days, Llanelly was a thrilling place to live and many Welshmen made their fortunes under the Australian sun.

A neighbouring mining town, Tarnagulla, enjoyed a similar boom. In 1868, four Welsh business partners (all named John) secured land on Poverty Reef, a place that defied its name. They unearthed one of the most valuable quartz gold deposits in the world, and the town that grew around it was one of opulence and excitement. Ladies were lowered into the mine in their finery and invited to chip out as much gold as they could carry. Millionaires were made, and Tarnagulla flourished, growing even larger and grander than Llanelly.

No gold rush lasts forever. By the late nineteenth century, yields dwindled, and both towns began to fade. Today, Tarnagulla is a quiet village of 150 residents, although it attracts visitors with its historic buildings and recreational prospecting. Llanelly lies almost desolate, with just a handful of houses, an empty bank, and a cemetery of headstones bearing Welsh names. The population has plummeted from 20,000 in the 1860s to just 62. Rusty train tracks run through the village, leading to nowhere.

Little remains of the mines themselves. A few brave souls still occasionally enter, searching for history rather than gold. These self-proclaimed mine-shaft chasers unearth clay pipes, boots and other relics, shedding new light on the little-known legacy of Victoria's gold mines.

VANISHING
CULTURAL
PRACTICE

# Ripped off: Papua New Guinea's sacred bark cloth

**Location:**
Bark cloth-making communities, Oro Province, southeastern Papua New Guinea

**Threat:**
Appropriation

Deep in the rainforests of Papua New Guinea's Oro Province, a traditional tattooed fabric called *tapa* is made from the bark of the mulberry tree. The bark is beaten and soaked until soft and malleable, then dried and smoothed out to create a material not unlike parchment paper. Finally, the cloth is tattooed with a paint-like dye made from bark, which varies from crimson to earthy brown, depending on the age of the tree.

For centuries, Oro men and women have worn *tapa* as traditional attire for dances and rituals, and exchanged the cloth in ceremonies. Each clan has a unique design, featuring geometric patterns and motifs that represent its history and identity. Passed through generations, *tapa* designs are sacred vessels of stories, ceremonies and ancestral knowledge. Within the Oro province, it is considered deeply offensive for a clan to use another clan's design without permission.

However, the deep connection between ancient *tapa* designs and the Oro people is not always respected by outsiders. *Tapa* designs have been appropriated by non-Oro designers and, in recent years, they have increasingly appeared on mass-produced t-shirts, bags and dresses. During the pandemic, stolen patterns were even reproduced on face masks. These imitations, sold without recognition or royalties, reduce sacred designs to decorative trinkets.

Losing authentic *tapa* to commercialisation would sever an intimate link between the Oro people and their land, diluting generations of stories, symbols and knowledge. Currently, there is no law to protect traditional *tapa* designs, but Oro's governor is exploring how to patent the designs that are unique to that province. Local artisans also advocate for intellectual property protections, fighting to keep sacred *tapa* in the hands of the Oro people and rooted in the rainforests of the Oro province.

# Polar regions

# On thin ice: Precarious polar bear habitats

For nearly 50 years, scientists have been using satellites to monitor the floating sea ice in the Arctic, and their findings make for troubling reading. The ice is shrinking dramatically in both its extent (the area of ocean it covers) and its thickness, with an average loss of thirteen percent per decade since 1979. What has truly alarmed experts is not the change in the sea ice itself, or even the fact it is declining, but the speed at which it has occurred. In the past, these types of adjustments took place over thousands of years; now they are happening in a matter of decades.

**Location:**
Arctic regions: Alaska (USA), Canada, Greenland, northern Norway and northern Russia

**Threat:**
Climate change

The reduction in summer ice has sped up significantly since the early 2000s, with the extent hitting a near historic low in 2024. Land ice on the surrounding islands and land-masses is melting too. Some of the smaller ice caps have already disappeared and Greenland is locked in an ongoing battle against coastal erosion. Beyond the Arctic regions, sea ice plays a vital role in our global ecosystem, acting as a vast, natural air conditioner and regulating Earth's climate and weather.

The loss of sea ice is especially devastating for polar bears, who rely on it to hunt. Polar bears live in the Arctic regions of the United States (Alaska), Canada, Greenland, Norway and Russia. Together, scientists from these five territories track polar bear numbers, and their data reveals that several populations are decreasing. The Southern Beaufort Sea bear population is estimated to have plummeted by 40 percent between 2001 and 2010.

No one knows precisely what the future holds for the Arctic and its precious furry inhabitants, but we won't have to wait long to find out. A 2024 study by researchers at the Universities of Gothenburg and Colorado Boulder predicts that the Arctic Ocean could experience its first ice-free day before 2030.

# Burned out: Norway's last Arctic coal mine

**Location:**
Gruve 7 coal mine, approximately 15km southeast of Longyearbyen town, Svalbard archipelago, northern Norway

**Threat:**
Closure

In the unending darkness of the polar night, a flood-lit monument rises from the snow. It honours the many miners who have died working in this unforgiving place, in the Svalbard archipelago, since 1916.

The memorial, called *The Miner*, stands in the remote town of Longyearbyen, still home to miners who work at Norway's last Arctic coal mine. Gruve 7 has operated for almost 50 years, managed by mining company Store Norske. Miners put their lives in each others' hands every time they descend into the cramped, dark tunnels, where the air hangs heavy with coal dust and the temperature is below freezing.

Norway's only coal-powered plant, in Longyearbyen, closed in 2023 as part of a move to greener alternatives. The transition prompted Store Norske to schedule the closure of Gruve 7 for 2025. The closure aims to reduce carbon dioxide emissions in the fragile, rapidly changing Arctic, but it also risks weakening the soul of a century-old mining community. The long mining tradition is a deep source of pride for Longyearbyen's families, and the cornerstone of the community's identity.

For Gruve 7's last generation of miners, grief for the end of an era is turning to anxiety about the future. Some in Longyearbyen are apprehensive about the wider implications of Norway ceasing coal mining on Svalbard, as it could leave Russia as the only nation with mining operations in the region.

Longyearbyen's community is adjusting to a future shaped by tourism, research and renewable energy, rather than coal. As their environment shifts, families will draw on the resilience and unity forged over generations in the mine to carry them forward.

# Breaking point: Antarctica's collapsing ice shelves

**Location:**
Ice shelves surrounding much of Antarctica, notably Conger-Glenzer Ice Shelf, East Antarctica

**Threat:**
Collapse

In March 2022, the Conger-Glenzer Ice Shelf – a slab of ice the size of Rome – shattered into fragments which dispersed into the Southern Ocean. Antarctic ice shelves are huge platforms of ice attached to the continent. Critically, they act like corks, holding back immense ice sheets which, scientists warn, contain enough ice to raise global sea levels by 58 metres if they were all to melt.

In 2024, scientists studying satellite images reported that the Conger-Glenzer Ice Shelf had been thinning for over two decades. Gradual structural weakening, caused by ocean warming and atmospheric changes, left it vulnerable to extreme weather. In 2022, strong winds and swells hastened its final collapse.

The disintegration of the Conger-Glenzer Ice Shelf was particularly striking because the final collapse took just a few days. Its location, in East Antarctica, was also highly unusual. Over the past few decades, around ten ice shelves have disintegrated in West Antarctica and the Antarctic Peninsula – regions more vulnerable to warming. East Antarctica, however, has long been considered reasonably stable. Conger-Glenzer was the first ice shelf collapse to be observed there. The event challenged assumptions about the region's resilience, raising concern among scientists that the collapse may signal broader instability.

Other major ice shelves are at risk, including the Larsen C Ice Shelf, part of the Antarctic Peninsula, which has experienced significant thinning and calving. If these shelves collapse, the glaciers behind them will flow freely into the ocean, accelerating sea-level rise. Scientists warn that the disappearance of ice shelves is a stark warning about climate change, and possibly even the start of a future we are not prepared for.

# Crunch time: Greenland's frozen city

**Location:**
Camp Century, 30m beneath Greenland's northwestern ice sheet

**Threat:**
Ice sheet dynamics

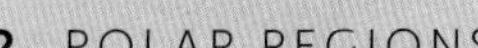

The resurfacing of an intentionally hidden place can have unsettling consequences. Around 30 metres beneath Greenland's thick ice sheet lies the remains of Camp Century, a United States Cold War military base built in 1959 as part of Project Iceworm. The camp was designed as a secret missile storage facility and a safe haven in case of nuclear war. Inside its labyrinth of tunnels, 200 soldiers lived in prefabricated huts with heat, light, and access to shops, a cinema and a science lab. The camp was abandoned in 1967, when maintaining it in harsh Arctic conditions proved impractical.

In 2024, while conducting radar studies over Greenland's ice sheet, NASA scientists inadvertently detected the forgotten city under the ice. The discovery was as troubling as it was fascinating. Although the nuclear reactor was removed after Camp Century's closure, the biological, chemical and radioactive waste – believed to weigh as much as 30 passenger planes – remains buried.

The US military assumed the toxic material would be preserved for eternity by the Arctic's perpetual freeze. However, recent climate models suggest melting ice could soon release these pollutants into the ocean, creating a potential environmental catastrophe. Who would bear responsibility for the escape of hazardous waste is itself a thorny issue, given that Camp Century was US-run at a time when Greenland, now self-governing, was under Danish administration.

President Trump's controversial claim that he intends to purchase Greenland from Denmark has reignited global interest in the country. For scientists, Camp Century provides valuable insights into ice sheet changes, while for politicians, its reemergence raises complex questions about how to respond when the past refuses to stay buried.

# Snowed under: Mawson's Huts

**Location:**
Mawson's Huts, Cape Denison, Commonwealth Bay, Antarctica, 3000km south of Hobart

**Threat:**
Extreme weather

In the frostbitten wilderness of Antarctica's Commonwealth Bay, there is an unexpected slice of civilization. Four prefabricated pine structures, encased in snow and ice, protrude from the plateau. Known as Mawson's Huts, they served as the base for the 1911–14 Australasian Antarctic Expedition, led by geologist and explorer Douglas Mawson. This is one of just six surviving sites from the Heroic Era of Antarctic Exploration, which began in the late nineteenth century and ended with Shackleton's death in 1922.

While the men of Mawson's expedition are long gone, their refuge has survived over a century of earth's most punishing conditions. For starters, Mawson's Huts are situated in one of the world's windiest places. Katabatic winds (icy downhill blasts) batter the structures at more than 200 kilometres per hour, in places reducing the timber walls to a thickness of less than one millimetre.

Slowly, the Antarctic continent is reclaiming the huts. Snow has pushed its way inside and frost clings to the corners of every room. Inside Mawson's Hut, the building that served as living quarters for eighteen men, it looks almost as if Mawson and his team have just stepped out. Simple wooden shelves sag under the weight of food tins, their labels faded and peeling. On a bunk, a half-burned candle in a tin sits beside an open book. On the bedside ledge, a cracked frame holds a faded photograph of a loved one.

The Australian government and non-profit organizations have funded various expeditions to excavate, document and repair Mawson's Huts. However, conservationists can only work in short stints and it's a costly business. Raising funds for expeditions is an ongoing challenge. Very few will ever step into Mawson's Hut, but a replica on Hobart waterfront offers a glimpse into the explorer's world and the chance to help fund critical conservation.

# Outer space

VANISHING
CULTURAL
PRACTICE

# The final frontier: Humanity's heritage on the Moon

**Location:**
Apollo 11 landing site, Tranquility Base, The Moon

**Threat:**
Lack of regulation

Throughout human history, we have gazed at the Moon in wonder, a shared fascination that peaked on 20 July 1969, when 650 million people watched Neil Armstrong become the first man to step onto its surface.

The *Apollo 11* landing site, known as Tranquility Base, is peppered with around 100 artefacts related to that iconic moment, including the landing module, scientific instruments and Armstrong's iconic boot print. The site has been well preserved by the absence of wind and flowing water on the moon. Now, as a new age of space exploration dawns, driven by the burgeoning commercial space industry, questions are being raised about protecting these historic traces of the first lunar landing.

Intriguingly, the World Monuments Fund (WMF) added the Moon to its 2025 list of heritage sites facing major challenges. The Fund warns that exploitative behaviour, such as souvenir gathering, by future commercial missions could compromise the Moon's cultural – as well as natural – landscape. Although NASA has published guidelines about sustainable lunar exploration, they are unenforceable. As a celestial object owned by no one, the Moon is ungoverned and law cannot be imposed on it.

In 2023, an international committee was formed to promote the preservation of humanity's heritage in space, but there is currently no binding agreement to preserve historic sites on the Moon. The WMF is calling for international collaboration to protect the lunar legacy. There is a precedent for this in the Antarctic Treaty System, which safeguards heritage that lies beyond the jurisdiction of any nation or governing body. Sceptics argue there are more pressing issues in space exploration than defending outer-space heritage, but with more companies setting their sights on the Moon, the WMF insists the time to act is now.

# Credits

## ABOUT THE AUTHOR

Amy Hopkins is a travel writer and award-winning editor with over a decade's experience in telling stories from around the world. A former travel magazine journalist, she's spent the past four years on staff at Rough Guides. *Vanishing Places* is her first book, and she's already halfway through her next.


## ACKNOWLEDGEMENTS

With thanks to all who shared their stories. And to N – thank you for vanishing with our children on Saturday mornings so I could write in peace.


## SOURCES

Each of the 100 stories in this book, though concise, draws on a diverse array of sources, from academic studies to conversations between the author and local people.

Rough Guides and the author acknowledge the many journalists, researchers, scientists and community members across the world whose work and words have informed *Vanishing Places* – with particular thanks to the following institutions:

- BBC
- *The Diplomat*
- *El País*
- *The Financial Times*
- *Forbes*
- *The Guardian*
- *The Independent*
- *Le Monde*
- *National Geographic*
- *New Scientist*
- *The New York Times*
- Radar Africa
- Reuters
- *Smithsonian Magazine*
- *The Sydney Morning Herald*
- *The Telegraph*
- *The Times*
- UNESCO
- United Nations
- *The Washington Post*
- World Monuments Fund
- WWF (World Wide Fund for Nature)

Scan the QR code for a complete list of sources and further reading suggestions:

**Rough Guides Vanishing Places**
Editor: Sarah Clark
Author: Amy Hopkins
Picture Manager: Tom Smyth
Production Operations Manager: Katie Bennett
Publishing Technology Manager: Rebeka Davies
Head of Publishing: Sarah Clark
Photo credits: Adobe Stock 6/7, 53, 102/103, 155, 190, 207; Alamy 5, 8/9, 10/11, 12, 13, 14/15, 27, 28/29, 34/35, 36, 38, 42, 44, 46/47, 56, 57, 64, 70/71, 72, 78, 79, 83, 86, 87, 88, 90/91, 99, 100, 105, 112/113, 114, 115, 120, 121, 122/123, 135, 138, 140, 144, 145, 160/161, 170/171, 172, 174/175, 176, 177, 178/179, 182, 183, 184, 192, 197, 198/199, 201, 202, 204/205, 208, 210/211, 214, 215; Bienvenido Velasco/EPA-EFE/Shutterstock 74/75; Dave Decker/ZUMA Press Wire/Shutterstock 82; Egmont Strigl/imageBROKER/Shutterstock 134; Igor Kovalenko/EPA/Shutterstock 142/143; Jeff Ernst/Guardian /eyevine 80/81; John Angelillo/UPI/Shutterstock 77; Kevin Schafer/Avalon 43; Khaled Elfiqi/EPA-EFE/Shutterstock 95; Martina Katz/imageBROKER/Shutterstock 96/97; Mattinbgn 200; Michael Nigro/Pacific Press/Shutterstock 76; Muhammad Ashar 166; New York Times/Redux/eyevine 62, 68/69, 168, 169; Newscom/Avalon 188/189; Public domain 212/213, 216/217, 218; Shutterstock editorial 50/51; Shutterstock 2, 16, 18/19, 20/21, 22, 23, 24, 26, 30/31, 32, 37, 40/41, 48/49, 52, 54/55, 58, 60, 61, 84/85, 92/93, 94, 98, 104, 106/107, 108, 109, 110, 116, 118/119, 124, 125, 128, 130/131, 132/133, 136/137, 139, 146/147, 148, 149, 152, 154, 156/157, 158, 162, 163, 164/165, 180/181, 186, 187, 191, 194/195, 209; Simon Townsley/Panos Pictures 126/127; Victor Moriyama/New York Times/Redux/eyevine 66/67; William Widmer/Redux /eyevine 63; WSL/Zuma Press/Avalon 196; Xinhua/Shutterstock 150/151, 159
Cover credits: Maldives **iStock**


First Edition 2025
ISBN: 9781835292761
Printed by Finidr in Czech Republic

A catalogue record for this book is available from the British Library.


**DISTRIBUTION**
UK, Ireland and Europe
Apa Publications (UK) Ltd; mail@roughguides.com
United States and Canada
Two Rivers; ips@ ingramcontent.com
Australia and New Zealand
Woodslane; info@woodslane.com.au
Worldwide
Apa Publications (UK) Ltd; mail@roughguides.com
**SPECIAL SALES, CONTENT LICENSING AND COPUBLISHING**
Rough Guides can be purchased in bulk quantities at discounted prices. We can create special editions, personalized jackets and corporate imprints tailored to your needs.
mail@roughguides.com; http://roughguides.com
**EU REPRESENTATIVE**
LOGOS EUROPE, 9 rue Nicolas Poussin, 17000, LA ROCHELLE, France
Contact@logoseurope.eu; +33 (0) 667937378

# Index